A Fast Platform for
Interactive E-Learning Systems

Ondřej Havel

Dissertation, Universität Passau

Erstgutachter: Prof. Dr. Franz Lehner
Zweitgutachter: Prof. Dr. Peter Kleinschmidt
Tag der Disputation: 13. Dezember 2013

Bibliografische Information der Deutschen Nationalbibliothek

Die Deutsche Nationalbibliothek verzeichnet diese Publikation in der
Deutschen Nationalbibliografie; detaillierte bibliografische Daten sind
im Internet über http://dnb.d-nb.de abrufbar.

ISBN 978-3-8325-3636-7

Logos Verlag Berlin GmbH
Comeniushof, Gubener Str. 47,
10243 Berlin
Tel.: +49 (0)30 42 85 10 90
Fax: +49 (0)30 42 85 10 92
INTERNET: http://www.logos-verlag.de

Preface

The Free Open Source Software (FOSS) has fascinated me since the early 1990s. In that time there were only several isolated groups of enthusiasts working on various open projects. The rising expansion of global communication networks helps to synchronize the developers and to coordinate their efforts worldwide. At the same time, it also seems that the general public interest in the FOSS rises hand in hand with the continuing growth of the internet. Nowadays, there exists a reasonable open solution for almost every task and there are strong user communities around each popular project. It seems that the FOSS is also being intensively used as an essential part of various devices of everyday life like televisions, mobile phones, cars, trains, but even medical devices, hadron colliders, and many others.

Presently, there are also very competitive free alternatives available for exacting applications like operating systems, databases, various servers, and programming languages, which in suitable combination allow the implementation and subsequent operation of complex information systems.

Information systems have always been a major topic of business informatics. One particular information system type is e-learning platforms. E-learning refers to the use of information technologies in education with the intended supportive effect on learning and teaching. One of the broadly used FOSS implementations is Ilias. Ilias is a web-based learning management system which has been used during the past years at the Chair of Business Computing II at the University of Passau for various courses and served several thousands of students during that time.

This publication provides a closer look at the past experience with Ilias, reviews course evaluations, classifies reported problems and tries to identify their root causes in the system. The cause of the major problem, weak performance of servers with heavily attended courses, seems to lie in the software architecture.

As a result of this work, an alternative framework with a different architecture is proposed. This approach seems to be able to eliminate all major problems that occurred with the Ilias system. A working prototype of an alternative e-learning system was developed on top of this framework as a proof of concept. All features

1

that have been used within Ilias during the courses, have been also implemented within the prototype. Usability evaluation and several performance related measurements of the underling hardware indicate that the newly developed system could be used as a fully fledged e-learning alternative which requires less resources and is able to run on a substantially slower hardware.

Acknowledgements

I would like to thank to the stalwart supporter and the first supervisor of this thesis, Prof. Dr. Franz Lehner, for his support during the development and for his valuable feedback. A special thank goes to Prof. Dr. Peter Kleinschmidt for his kind cooperation.

There are many others whom I would also like to thank, mostly the authors and maintainers of all respective tools, modules, and libraries which were involved during the creation of this work. Some of them became mandatory and are required for proper operation of the software. This document was written at the Chair of Business Computing II[1] at the University of Passau.

---

[1]http://www.wi.uni-passau.de/

Contents

List of Figures

Listings

Nomenclature

AMF3	Action Message Format 3
API	Application Interface
ASN.1	Advanced Syntax Notation One
BER	Basic Encoding Rules
CGI	Common Gateway Interface
CLE	Collaboration and Learning Environment
CMS	Content Management System
CPAN	Comprehensive Perl Archive Network
CPU	Central Processing Unit
FOSS	Free Open Source Software
GNU	Unix-like computer operating system composed wholly of free software
GPL	GNU General Public License
GUI	Graphical User Interface
HTML	Hypertext Markup Language
HTTP	Hypertext Transfer Protocol
HTTPS	Hypertext Transfer Protocol Secure
IMDB	In-Memory Database
IP	Internet Protocol
IRC	Internet Relay Chat

ISO	International Organization for Standardization
LAMP	Linux (operating system), Apache HTTP Server, MySQL (database software), and PHP, Perl or Python
LCMS	Learning Content Management System
LDAP	Lightweight Directory Access Protocol
LMS	Learning Management System
MDI	Multiple Document Interface
MP3	MPEG-1 or MPEG-2 Audio Layer III
MXML	Macromedia eXtensible Markup Language
NGO	Non-governmental organization
noSQL	Not only SQL
OSI	Open Systems Interconnection Model
PC	Personal Computer
PDF	Portable Document Format
PER	Packed Encoding Rules
PHP	PHP: Hypertext Preprocessor, a recursive acronym
POSIX	Portable Operating System Interface
RAM	Random-Access Memory
RBAC	Role-Based Access Control
RIA	Rich Internet Application
SCORM	Sharable Content Object Reference Model
SDK	Software Development Kit
SMTP	Simple Mail Transfer Protocol
SQL	Structured Query Language
SWF	Small Webplatform Format
TCP	Transmission Control Protocol

UA	User Agent
UDP	User Datagram Protocol
UI	User Interface
VLE	Virtual Learning Environment
VoIP	Voice over IP
VRAM	Video Random Access Memory
W3C	World Wide Web Consortium
XML	Extended Markup Language
XSI	X/Open System Interfaces Extension, a supplementary specification to the Single UNIX Specification

Chapter 1

Introduction

1.1 Problem Description

The rapid evolution of new information technologies allows implementation of powerful web information systems which are able to process a large amount of incoming requests. Thanks to the internet each request can come from any arbitrary place on the Earth. Albeit the hardware prices have been falling continuously for several decades now and the price/performance ratio of the key computer components sinks similarly fast, there still often occur problems with the insufficient performance of some information systems running on a recent hardware with a higher amount of concurrent active clients.

Web e-learning systems represent one such type of information systems. In university environments they are widely used and often highly attended. In case that the online attendance of an e-learning system is sufficiently high, the e-learning system can also show symptoms of performance problems. Weak performance can be directly observed by the users, usually manifesting itself in form of a slower reaction time upon each user request. Longer waiting time lengthens the total time needed to accomplish a certain task within the system and it can also have a negative impact on the usability of the system.

In worst case, the waiting time can exceed the range of tolerance and discourages users from using the system. The next possibility is the complete system malfunction. The system may exit unexpectedly as a result of a software error or after exhausting all resources of the underlying operating environment. The shortage of resources can also arise from too many simultaneously active users. Each active user affects all other connected users reciprocally by consuming the computing time and other resources of the host system.

1.2 Motivation

Ilias [62] is a learning management system originally developed at the University of Cologne and released under the General Public License (GPL). The project has been developed as a free open source software (FOSS) since the year 2000. It is a very versatile software offering several different features for realisation of distant and blended learning, for communication, cooperation, and collaboration for projects and teams. It can be used as a knowledge base and a digital library in organizations, and it also includes an assessment environment which can be optionally used for the testing of the participants. A suitable combination of these features can provide a complete e-learning system complying with almost any structural and functional requirement. There are several hundreds of confirmed Ilias installations worldwide [86] including commercial organizations and institutions, schools, universities, etc.

At the University of Passau, at the Chair of Business Computing II, a common midrange server entirely equipped with FOSS is used for providing e-learning services in multiple courses. The software system consists of various fundamental components: Debian operating system, Apache web server with PHP support, MySQL database, and finally Ilias learning management system. Past experience with this configuration has shown that during the times of a high attendance, the system experiences performance issues. Individual users recognize the performance problems as noticeably longer waiting times during the communication with the system.

The general assumption is that the presently used hardware with a slightly modified internal arrangement of the software equipment is able to serve even a larger number of simultaneous users offering the same service without the performance issues. The book describes the establishment of a suitable architecture and the implementation of a new generic framework for the general distributed data and event propagation suitable for specific kinds of information systems. For maximizing the performance, the framework utilizes computing power of the clients. Therefore, the rich internet application (RIA) concept is used. The book deals with the implementation of an e-learning prototype which includes all features which were used in the past electronic courses with Ilias.

The prototype, developed as a proof of concept, is compared with the currently used Ilias system during a simulation. The simulation is conducted in order to show the performance advantage of the prototype. The prototype and the Ilias systems are tested by a special network application which replicates the critical situation when a large amount of users interacts with the system simultaneously.

Because the prototype is an application written practically from scratch, usability of its user interface was evaluated repeatedly during the development. Although there were still several problems identified in the user interface, the testing with real users has shown that the prototype can be used as a fully fledged alternative. Additionally, thanks to the RIA concept, several usability problems of Ilias with the interactivity and interface feedback could have been eliminated.

The core framework also opens a way for a general update and extension of older information systems with a similar architecture but it also enables a rapid implementation of entirely new information systems. By suitable utilization of the framework, the critical parts of the system can be designed and implemented in a manner with a positive impact on the overall system performance.

1.3   Document Organization

Chapter 1 contains the introduction and describes the initial motivation for the development.

Chapter 2 presents electronic learning and outlines the state of the art of e-learning systems.

Chapter 3 introduces the basic definitions and properties of a generic system and related terms. It also deals with the basic principles of communication within a system. What is described are the elementary terms used for the system analysis. The analysis deals with special methods for computerized systems covering various techniques for data transformations and interchange.

Chapter 4 discusses common features and architecture of a web e-learning application and focuses on the typical communication endpoints within such systems. Ilias system is introduced, user experiences and results of multiple evaluations are summarized and used as starting points for the development of an alternative system.

Chapter 5 proposes an optimized communication framework designed for improved performance. The development of a new web e-learning prototype on top of this framework is described with major focus on its architecture with its key components and interfaces. Special software facilities are also mentioned. They include the client and server in-memory databases in their specific Perl and ActionScript implementations and the implementation of the distributed content caching mechanism.

Chapter 6 presents a direct comparison of the prototype with the original Ilias system in a specific configuration as presented in chapter 4. Problems identified in the evaluation are reused to summarize functional differences and improvements of the new system. A performance test is conducted using a special scenario simulating the real user behaviour. The purpose of this comparison is to show the increased system performance, lower hardware requirements, and the ability to handle more simultaneous connections.

Chapter 7 provides a summary of past development efforts and proposes several next possibilities for further extensions.

The appendices are addressing the preparation, installation, configuration, and maintenance processes of all respective system components.

Appendix A summarizes the major features and individual controls of the client. The most distinctive interfaces, the basic learning interface and the administrative interface are described in separate chapters.

Appendix B provides elementary information on the prerequisites of the server software and its preparation, on various configuration possibilities and finally on the operation of the server.

Chapter 2

Electronic Learning

This chapter briefly introduces electronic learning (e-learning) including learning theories, methods, and used technologies.

2.1 Learning and Learning Theories

Lehner defines learning [44] as an information transforming process which leads to a change of mental structures. This change results afterwards in a different reaction which is initiated by the same stimulus. There are several general epistemological learning theories: objectivism, pragmatism, and constructivism [76]. Connectivism [43] represents a complementary theory to older approaches working not only with *"know how"* and *"know what"*, but additionally extending this space with the *"know where"* dimension. The following list briefly describes each theory:

- **Objectivism/Behaviorism** assumes that human beings have a direct access to the (external) reality through own preceptors which then create knowledge in their minds (internal), simultaneously is the human perceived as a black box system. What happens inside during the learning process remains unknown, emphasis is given on the observable and measurable behaviour [76].

- **Pragmatism/Cognitivism** pictures the active knowledge development from a successful encounter with own experience. Learning is viewed as an active process that occurs within the human with emphasis on the structure and organization to facilitate the optimal information processing [76].

- **Constructivism/Interpretivism** describes how individuals build a new knowledge upon existing experience through accommodation and assimilation. With assimilation, a new knowledge is added to the present base, accommodation means a process where a failure leads to learning [76].

- **Connectivism** assumes that the knowledge is due to the big and still growing amount spread over in multiple systems rather than concentrated in minds of single individuals. These systems can be accessed by people participating in a learning process and together, they create a network. One drawback is that the individual can not have the full control over the learning process because the network represents a quickly changing dynamic system. Connectivism is also called as the *"learning theory for the digital age"* [68, 45].

2.2 Learning Methods

In order to achieve the desired learning effect, there are several learning methods that can be used. Kahiigi et al. [37] classify present methods in the following main categories:

- **Traditional learning** refers to sessions where teachers and students are present at the same time on the same place. The teacher acts as the primary information source.

- **E-learning** refers to the use of information technology with supportive effect on learning. E-learning includes a broad variety of functions and possibilities and in its extreme form can substitute traditional learning completely.

- **Blended learning** actively combines various traditional methods with e-learning in order to maximize the learning potential of individual students.

2.3 E-Learning Technologies

The progress of e-learning is tightly bound with the evolution of the underlying hardware systems. There are several major categories that can be identified with the technological milestones that were reached in the past. Starting in early 1990s with the adoption of the compact disc which offered superior capacity at a very low cost. Similar changes and trends can be observed with the growing availability of broadband internet connection and wireless mobile devices. Each milestone opened several new possibilities also for e-learning applications. Kahiigi et al. [37] also provide an overview of various e-learning technologies:

- **CD and DVD media** have been used for delivering study material in distance courses. The use of physical media encourages completely independent learning. Participants learn using special applications and they do not need network access.

- **Learning Management System (LMS)** is a specific kind of information systems and processes that are directly involved in learning and learning management. The primary purpose is to provide an online and universally accessible interface. Therefore, the LMSs are usually implemented as web information systems. Interactivity is mostly defined as mutual or reciprocal action or influence, where more than one entity communicate. Interaction and communication are the essential features of the most recent LMSs. There are several other confusing abbreviations used for similar systems. Other commonly used abbreviations are the collaboration and learning environment (CLE) and the virtual learning environment (VLE).

- **Content Management Systems (CMS)** are developed to facilitate the creation, management, and organization of a generic content in a centralized environment. A subset of CMS functionality is usually also included in the LMS systems for creation and manipulation with the course data. In the past, another denomination, learning content management system (LCMS) was used to distinguish systems with at least some or more advanced content management functions.

2.4 Popular Free Systems

There are several e-learning systems available as FOSS. Hauger et al. [33] provide an extensive overview of commercial and free systems in 2007 and also states that it is almost impossible to set up a complete list. Following survey provides a brief list of most frequently used free e-learning systems as listed on Freecode [85] and other publicly available software indexes.

- **Ilias** is a platform for web-based training. It is being developed at the University of Cologne, in Germany, using PHP and MySQL. It has been available since September 2000 as open software software under the GPL. The system's core is an authoring tool for creating courses. Other main components include personal desktops, a mail system, newsgroups, a group system, and system administration.

- **Moodle** is a learning management system for producing internet-based course web sites. It is written in PHP and is easy to install and use on Linux, Windows, Mac OS X, SunOS, BSD, and Netware 6. It has been designed to support modern pedagogies based on social constructionist theory, and includes activity modules such as forums, chats, resources, journals, quizzes, surveys, choices, workshops, glossaries, lessons, and assignments. It has been translated into over 70 languages, with more on the way, and supports the popular SCORM standard for content packaging. Moodle is being used by a growing number of universities, schools, and independent teachers for distance education or to supplement face-to-face teaching.

- **OpenOLAT** is a learning management system used by universities, schools, and companies to deliver e-learning content, to do testing and assessment, and to work collaboratively in various learning scenarios.

- **Sakai** includes many of the features common to LMS, including document distribution, a gradebook, discussion, live chat, assignment uploads, and online testing. Sakai is a web cross-platform software written in Java.

- **Chamilo** is an e-learning and collaboration platform. Chamilo is currently used by more than 460,000 students around the world. Governments, private companies, public and private universities, NGOs, and other types of organizations use the Chamilo software suite to manage activities from simple live training to full distant learning, certification, and staff selection. Chamilo runs on PHP.

- **Claroline** (classroom online) is a collaborative learning environment that allows teachers or educational institutions to create and administer courses through the web. The system provides group management, forums, document repositories, a calendar, chat, assignment areas, links, and user profile administration in a single, highly integrated package. It has been translated into 28 languages. Claroline runs on PHP.

- **BigBlueButton** is a web conferencing system that focuses on usability, modularity, and clean design, both for the user and developer. It implements real-time sharing of voice, web cams, desktops, slides, and chat messages to provide remote students with a high-quality learning experience. Unlike other conferencing systems, the desktop sharing works on Mac OS X, Unix, and PC computers, and there is no hard-coded limit on the number of simultaneous web cams. Unlike prior systems, a special streaming media server is utilized for the real-time collaboration.

2.5   Evolution of E-Learning

Present computer technologies can be used for implementation and operation of very versatile and powerful e-learning systems. Though the universality requirement can also be seen as a constraint. Development of a system that can be used almost anywhere, limits the technological portfolio substantially and at the moment the web clearly seems to be the predestined target environment. The progress of web technology also opens new ways for innovative software and together with powerful hardware represents a great challenge for the development of new systems.

Chapter 3

Basic Terms and Definitions

This chapter introduces generic terms like the system, its basic features, heterogeneous and hybrid environments, interfaces, and specific communication protocols for computerized systems.

3.1 System and its Structure

The following chapter provides a general definition of a system as introduced by Novák et al. [54]. The system is characterized as any organized formation of physical, chemical, biological, social, or informational units, components, and elements, which are able to fulfill one or more purposeful functions.

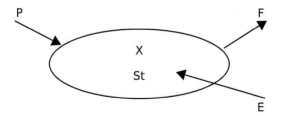

Figure 3.1: System and its basic properties.

Figure 3.1 shows a formal system with the following properties:

- set of target functions implemented and realized by the system, $F = f_1, \dots, f_i$

- system structure (topology) St describing the internal arrangement

- vector of system parameters $X = x_1, \ldots, x_j$ describing the current system state

- vector of independent variables $P = p_1, \ldots, p_k$ used as the input of the system functions

- E, the set of outer environmental variables with influence on the system

The time t is usually the one of the most important environmental variables for technical systems, which means that the topology, the system parameters, and the independent variables can be understood as time functions. The book works with the assumption that for technical systems, the time variable is absolutely independent. The independence means that the time is a real, scalar, continuous variable, whose value can only grow.

3.1.1 System Life Curve

The set of all possible combinations of states X during the time when the system is working properly is called the region of acceptability and will be marked as R_A. The system is malfunctioning whenever the vector X leaves the R_A. Figure 3.2 shows an idealized example. The region of acceptance does not have to be a continuous set.

The system life curve Ψ is a thought trajectory of the system state vector X in time t (also $X = \Psi(t)$). For sufficiently large value of t, the life trajectory of a closed technical system always leaves the region of acceptability R_A irreversibly [55].

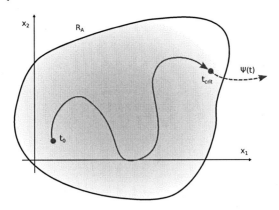

Figure 3.2: System life curve.

3.1.2 Reliability and Lifespan

Novák et al. [54] define reliability, lifespan, and safety as the major secondary characteristic of a system.

The system reliability can be expressed as a probability that the vector describing the current system state will not deviate from required value more than the permitted deviation rate ΔF.

Related to the acceptance area, the reliability can be expressed as a probability $R(X, t)$ that for a given time interval the system life curve $\Psi(t)$ will not leave the acceptance area R_A. Accordingly, the lifespan is the total time till the life curve leaves the system acceptance area.

Achievement of high reliability is one of the most important engineering tasks. There are several general methods which can be used for increasing the lifespan of a generic system. The following list provides a short overview:

- **Technological methods** consist in increasing the quality and reliability of the individual system parts. In terms of software development the reliability refers to the overall quality of the system's software. Utas [74] states: *"Although bug-free operation is the goal of an extreme system, it cannot be achieved in practice. Once again, cost, time to market, and the impossibility of testing all possible scenarios preclude it. The question, therefore is, how many bugs are acceptable."*

- **Backup methods** are based on multiple equivalent instances of the target system. In case of a failure of one system instance, its functionality can be taken over by an another working instance ideally instantly. In computerized systems, the backup often takes place at a lower application level with focus on duplicating of the essentials. The truly essential and unique part in standardized software is the data. In this case, a system recovery often means a short outage for the data restoration.

- **Structural methods** focus on improving of the internal rearrangement of the components in an existing system and trying to achieve such a configuration that the parts with least performance or reliability impact the target functions only minimally. The overall performance of a complex system consisting of multiple function blocks is often negatively affected by the underperformed communication interfaces among the components. The interfaces have to be revised and eventually substituted if no further internal rearrangement is possible.

- **Predictive methods** are used to monitor and estimate the position of the current system state $\Psi(t)$ with a sufficient time advance. In critical cases,

31

the $\Psi(t)$ trajectory can be adjusted by an external intervention so that it does stays in the R_A for further time. For computer systems there are several monitoring tools available. With help of these tools, the t_{crit} can be estimated for individual system parts and in an ideal case, the system administrator can take necessary steps in order to keep the system running, not leaving the R_A.

3.1.3 Heterogeneous Systems

Various distinct and logically separable parts can be understood as a heterogeneous system. These parts, also called components or function blocks, interact together through interfaces. An interface is a place at which two independent systems exchange energy or matter in various forms. Figure 3.3 shows an idealized heterogeneous system with several function blocks. In case that the components share the same target functions, such group of components can be also called the system alliance. In terms of computerized systems, a cloud consisting of multiple servers is an example of such an alliance.

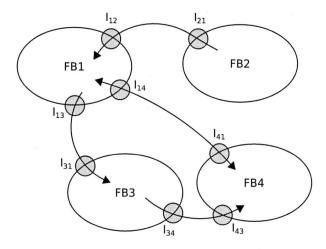

Figure 3.3: Idealized heterogeneous system.

3.1.4 Hybrid Systems

The classic concept of a hybrid system [3] defines it as a special kind of a heterogeneous system with its dynamics realized partly in the continuous and partly in the discrete time domain. It is also usually possible to find subsystems working in both domains on different hierarchical levels within the system.

Novák et al. [55] state that *"during the course of its existence human society has generated various artificial systems. These have subsequently changed their role from auxiliary to necessary. At present, we cannot exist without the use of majority of them, nevertheless, we still complain about these systems and dream of life without them. Frankly speaking, the main real reason for our complaints about artificial systems can be seen – disregarding their frequent misuse – in their unsatisfactory operation reliability and safety and also in unwanted or unexpected side effects of their use and existence."*

3.1.5 Human as a System Component

In purely technical systems the operator controlling the whole system or its substantial part is often a human. The human element included in the system seems also to be the weakest and the most problematic one regarding reliability and safety. Considering the reliability or the data interchange rate, the human usually looses in a direct comparison with a purely technical system. Nevertheless, for obvious reasons the human element plays an indispensable role also in the management of information systems.

3.1.6 Human Interfaces

Stary [70] describes several different interface implementations for data interchange between an information system and a human. He also defines an interactive system as a specially combined social-technical system consisting of a hardware, software, and a human. For purpose of this work, the hardware and software are represented by a recent desktop computer with installed operating system and a web browser. The web browser represents the host environment for the client application and its graphical user interface.

3.1.7 Window Manager

Desktop computer systems view the entire screen as a working area. With help of a window manager is this area split in working fragments – windows, through which individual applications can interact with the user. The user gains control of windows within the window manager. Most window managers use the concept of overlapping windows. This concept was developed as a key component of the graphical user interface, enabling computer users to simultaneously manage multiple contexts [75]. Although window managers are widely used in desktop environments, completely different workspace visualisation approaches are preferred on modern mobile devices, mostly due to the restricted display size and the limited touch control precision.

3.2 Interprocess Communication

This chapter deals with mutual communication of separate processes in the underlying operating system. A process is a fundamental concept to all operating systems. According to Gray [30], it is a dynamic entity scheduled and controlled by the operating system. It is a specific virtual subsystem containing a program code, needed resources, and a state information which is needed by the operating system in order to actually manage the process. Unix operating systems represent an environment, where multiple processes are able to run concurrently and at any given point in time it seems that they are running simultaneously. But that is only an illusion because in fact, it is the operating system who switches the processes in a way that it seems that they run simultaneously. Each process is seemingly able to acquire system resources like operating memory or access to a peripheral device without restrictions and without being aware of existence of other processes which is again an illusion as these requirements are completely handled by the operating system.

The following list discusses different methods which can be used for data interchange between two processes or threads. Main focus was on efficient methods which allow to exchange big amounts of data in a reasonable time. Some other standard methods, like file sharing with the use of the filesystem, are considered unsuitable and are not mentioned in the list. The list primarily focuses on methods typical for Unix systems. In different operating environments, the same effect can be achieved using similar methods usually with slightly different properties and names.

- **Signal** is a basic mechanism intended to provide rudimentary control over a process and does not deal with data interchange directly. Signals are often used for time interval measurements, process interruptions, and notifications. For example, a running process can be notified after its configuration file was changed in order to reload the file and reflect the configuration changes.

- **Pipe** is one the most elementary constructs for interprocess communication in Unix environments. The `pipe` command creates two file descriptors. One exclusively for writing and one for reading. The pair is typically created within one process which is then split into two processes using the `fork` command. One file descriptor is then passed to the newly created process and mutual communication can start. Pipe basically provides only one way communication channel. For communicating in both directions, two `pipe` calls are mandatory.

- **FIFO** (First In First Out) queues are created by the `mkfifo` command. They are similar to Unix pipes with the difference that there is an initial string reference required for the creation. This reference is represented in the file system as a special entry in the directory structure. The next difference is that a named pipe can exist in the filesystem for a longer time even if it is not used. The filesystem entry can be then deleted like an ordinary file.

- **Unix Domain Protocols** (UDP) are not an actual protocol suite but a way of performing communication on a single host using same application interface (API) that is used for mutual communication of remote hosts [72]. Generally, there are two major categories of Unix sockets – datagrams and streams. Datagrams, similarly to the UDP protocol [58] are intended for the interchange of small packets which are transmitted and read at once. The stream socket works then similarly to the Transmission Control Protocol (TCP) [60] which lacks the direct support of message delimitation. The delimitation mechanism is according to the application protocol either not needed or it has to be implemented additionally.

- **Message queues, semaphores, and shared memory** are methods for interprocess communication which are specified by the POSIX:XSI Extension and have their origins in the Unix System V interprocess communication as stated by Robbins [61]. Shared memory is a special memory region that can be accessed by multiple applications simultaneously. Shared memory can be utilized for mutual interprocess communication or to avoid data redundancy.

- The **mmap** is another POSIX compliant function that maps a file into memory and reduces the overhead for applications accessing this file. File operations for reading, writing, and seeking are simply substituted with the direct memory access. According to Gallmeister [27] is the `mmap` call generally preferred to shared memory mechanism because mapped memory does not stay persistent in the operating system after application exits.

3.3 Multithreaded Programming

The smallest unit of independently handled sequence of elementary instructions is a thread of execution. A thread is a special process created by an ordinary operating system process. Multiple threads can exist within one process and they are executed concurrently. There are several different implementations of threads. In some implementations, the threads are handled directly by the operating system, but threads can also exist within operating systems without the direct support of threading. There are multiple libraries with established APIs which can be used for the implementation of a multithreaded environment on different operating systems. Carver et al. [11] summarize multiple approaches for multithreaded programming in different environments.

The major advantage of threads over multiple cooperating processes is lower overhead during the mutual communication. Threads share most of their resources with other threads of the same process. Typically, the memory space and file descriptors. However, in order to avoid mutual collisions, there are several mechanisms which are used for access control and synchronization.

Butenhof [9] deals with POSIX compliant threaded programming and describes the elementary mutual exclusion mechanisms (mutexes) and advanced constructs like semaphores. In higher level programming languages like Perl, there are several modules dealing with multithreaded programming available. The basic implementation includes the elementary synchronization mechanisms as described by Stein [71], but there are also several modules implementing functionality for the interchange of complex data structures between processes and threads. This topic is broadly covered by Wainwright [77].

3.4 Network Communication

Cassel et al. [12] define computer network as a collection of mutually connected computers that are able to exchange messages and he also identifies the three main components required by a computer network:

- a transmission medium

- an interface between the medium and the computer

- software to drive the communication

In the end, this list of prerequisites can be further generalized and extended to the seven abstract layers resulting in the OSI reference model [6, 12].

3.4.1 Client/Server Systems

Web client/server systems use the TCP for data interchange. TCP provides continuous reliable delivery of endless byte streams in both communication directions. The underlying protocol is typically the Internet Protocol (IP) [59, 18] and both used together are known as TCP/IP.

The disadvantage of using endless streams is the lack of data delimitation during a subsequent exchange of multiple records of variable length within one connection [67]. The application has to insert additional markers in order to separate the records from each other. A simple encapsulation of a separate record is usually achieved by prepending the record with a header information containing the data length.

3.4.2 Hypertext Transfer Protocol

The Hypertext Transfer Protocol (HTTP) is an application protocol for distributed information systems as specified most recently in RFC 2616 [23]. The HTTP works as a request-response protocol [31] and it is usually used for the web content delivery between the browser (client) and the web server. The browser is a specific implementation on top of a generic user agent (UA) which is a library capable of communication with an HTTP server.

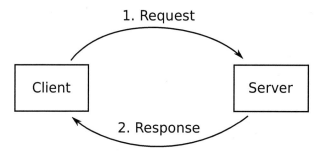

Figure 3.4: HTTP Transaction.

The HTTP/1.1 is a revision and ancestor of the original HTTP/1.0 as specified by RFC 1945 [5]. The major difference is that the HTTP/1.1 can handle multiple requests using one existing connection. The predecessor opens a new connection for each new request which can in many cases increase the communication overhead dramatically.

However, a spontaneous communication in the opposite direction from server to client is not practically possible and the request-response constraint remains the major problem also in HTTP/1.1. RFC 6202 [46] introduces HTTP Long Polling and HTTP Streaming in order to overcome this problem.

- **HTTP Long Polling**

    The server attempts to 'hold open' (not immediately reply to) each HTTP request, responding only when there are events to deliver. In this way, there

37

is always a pending request to which the server can reply for the purpose of delivering events as they occur, thereby minimizing the latency in message delivery.

- **HTTP Streaming**

  The server keeps a request open indefinitely; that is, it never terminates the request or closes the connection, even after it pushes data to the client.

Although these approaches sound very promising, the major problem is that there are practically no usable implementations available so far for relevant server and client components. Therefore, utilization of a custom additional connection without the request-response constraint seems presently to be the better choice regarding the development effort.

3.5 Session Connections

A session connection is a plain TCP/IP link between the client and the server which stays open for the whole session duration (time during which the user interacts with the system). Session connection works in true full-duplex mode so not only the client, who also initiates the connection, but also the server may send data completely spontaneously at any time. This also makes the logic used on both sides very similar. In case that the programming environments are the same, identical algorithms for data processing can be theoretically used on both sides. Each data arrival triggers an event, data are read and when a complete record is received, it is further processed.

Figure 3.5: Session connection.

3.6 Web Applications

Web application is a special kind of computer application that can be accessed by users over a network with a web browser which belongs to the standard software. Web browser interprets various input data formats which are primarily used for the implementation of user interfaces. Individual specifications of these formats

38

are supervised by the World Wide Web Consortium (W3C). Sosinsky [69] introduces the W3C as the central standards body for the World Wide Web which defines HTML and related standards, as well as protocols used by web servers.

The WebSocket Protocol specified in RFC 6455 [22] was introduced in 2011 as an open standard. It enables two-way communication between the client and the server. The goal of this technology is to provide a mechanism for browser-based applications that need a truly two-way communication channel with the server. HTML 5 and related standards were adopted by most browsers for mobile and desktop use [29]. Further evolution will allow the development of complex web applications utilizing session connections based exclusively on open W3C standards.

Up to this day the development of advanced web applications was possible using special frameworks. One of theses frameworks, the Flash, was not originally developed as an open standard. This framework has to be installed as an additional browser extension module. There are several different modules for the most popular browsers and there is also a version for Android devices. The history of the framework begins already in year 1994.

3.6.1 Rich Internet Applications

Rich Internet Applications (RIAs) are a sort of technical innovation on presentation layer and they are becoming strongly popular in the past years. The major purpose of a RIA framework is to provide a robust application layer. This layer enables the execution of code within the client. The client can also contain a part of logic. Thanks to the embedded logic, an extended functionality can be achieved which would not be with the classic thin client arrangement easily possible. Or at least the functionality would have to be handled by the server. From an architectural point of view, is this the major difference to the thin client, which can only display single web pages but do not contain any logic at all.

An effective coordination of application logic between the server and the client can have several positive effects like better application responsibility, interactivity, and overall better user experience. Another theoretical advantage is also the reduced server load, since after the migration of former server logic to the client, eventually only a little remains on the server.

Moore et al. [49] provide a comprehensive RIA summary. The typical prerequisite of a RIA is a special framework which usually exists in form of a modular extension. Such extension is additionally installed and becomes a part of the web browser. When a RIA is accessed, the extension is loaded and application can be executed. Nowadays, there are many different RIA frameworks and some of them, like HTML 5, are getting widely accepted and slowly standardized and they are getting directly implemented in major web browsers.

When the prototype development started in 2010, the Flex framework was chosen and it has been used since then. The following chapter briefly discusses the history and major features of this framework.

3.6.2 Apache Flex

The Apache Flex framework has a long history reaching back to the year 2004 [78]. In that time, Macromedia released the first version of the SDK. Since then, the framework underwent a rapid evolution, in 2005 Macromedia was acquired by Adobe which continued in the development of the framework. The whole suite (in that time Flex 3 SDK) was in 2008 released under the open source Mozilla Public License. The current version of the SDK is 4.9 which was released under the Apache License version 2.

The executable result which is produced by the SDK is called the Small Web-platform Format (SWF). It is a file which is downloaded by the web browser as part of a web page and subsequently executed by specific a browser extension which was installed previously. There are many alternatives, the best known from Adobe is called simply the Adobe Flash Player. The great advantage of Flash Player is its worldwide penetration [87] and high popularity among PC and mobile users.

Flex is based on ActionScript, an object-oriented language originally developed by Macromedia already in 1994. The language was originally developed for controlling simple graphic objects and vector animations. Later versions extended the functionality in order to allow the creation of more complex web applications. In its present version, ActionScript 3.0 supports scalar and complex data types, allows extensive control of peripheral devices, includes the direct support for XML and AMF3 data processing, and support for persistent client-to-server connections.

During the compilation process, Flex works with two input file formats. The MXML files have special format combining an XML description of the graphical user interface controls with code written in plain ActionScript. The native ActionScript code contains the logic for selected input events, for instance, for a button press, for arrival of data, etc.

The source files can not be directly executed by the client, they have to be compiled. First, the MXML descriptive part is translated into a regular Action-Script format with the mxmlc pre-compiler. In this process, code for all user interface elements is generated. Generated ActionScript files are then compiled altogether into the final SWF output. The SWF file is a compressed binary file containing bytecode which can be executed by the client extension module.

The advantage of Flex is a big amount of publicly available libraries for almost any task. There are several ActionScript implementations of window managers, cryptographic and miscellaneous libraries, some of them were used during the prototype development. Fain et al. [21] provide very useful surveys and comparisons of selected libraries for various tasks.

Chapter 4

E-Learning with Ilias

This chapter describes the general properties of a low cost e-learning solution with Ilias, its architecture and elementary features, discusses the results of evaluations of the past years, classifies the identified issues, and shows a real-world situation resulting in excessive waiting times.

4.1 Online E-Learning

Holmes et al. [34] summarize various definitions of e-learning into *"online access to learning resources, anywhere and anytime"*. An e-learning application, also called the learning management system, consists of multiple specific tools for the administration of user accounts, for the administration and work with the learning content, and for communication.

There are several possibilities where the learning and teaching processes can be set in. Synchronous learning in real-time can replicate most of the real-world situations like lectures and seminars. Such system requires the simultaneous presence of all participants during a time period. The audiovisual content is per streaming instantly distributed to all participants of the event. Bigbluebutton [2] is the one of such systems with primary a focus on content sharing in real-time.

Asynchronous systems, on the other hand, provide a library with ready-made learning content and enable completely independent learning at any time. In order to provide a feedback channel for course participants and administrators, they may also include suitable tools for mutual communication and instant messaging. An important part for estimation of the learning progress of individual participants is the assessment component. The assessment component is usually implemented as a test generator which creates random tests from pools of questions. Each participant can generate, answer, and review a test. Every individual step is handled completely automatically by the system. Properly prepared automated tests can be used as an indicator showing the rate of understanding of the learning content.

4.2 Web Portals

Term portal denotes a special, usually a dynamically generated web page which unifies the access to the associated resources of various kinds. Nowadays, the most spread approach of information exchange is based on the W3C specifications and related standards. HTML documents are represented by a text data containing actual human readable information and possible references to other HTML documents and resources. Learning portal aggregates a suitable set of HTML documents that fully or optionally support the students in their learning efforts. Portal structure is defined, created, and maintained by the administrators.

4.3 Present Implementation

At the time of writing, there are several learning portal products freely available as FOSS. Costa et al. [15] provide a comprehensive overview. Probably the best known and widely spread is Ilias [62] which is also being used for multiple courses at the language center and at the Chair of Business Computing II at the University of Passau in Germany. Every semester, there are up to approx. 1000 students using Ilias primarily or supplementary during their courses.

This chapter takes a closer look at the typical realization of an e-learning course with Ilias 4 and its features. The basic functionality is usually implemented similarly in concurrent FOSS web learning portals. Schäfer [65] states that the development of such a solution is a very complex task. He describes the fundamental software architecture and the hardware arrangement. Similar configurations can be often well identified in certain present web information systems.

The Ilias LMS is written in PHP and it is compliant with the recent W3C standards. The project was started in 1997. In that time, an average personal computer had only minimal resources and performance in comparison to today's standards. Correspondingly lesser possibilities and support for interactivity were included in the past W3C standards. Their rather slow and stepwise evolution probably also reflected in features that were implemented within Ilias.

Thanks to the open nature of HTML, web documents can be easily extended and they are able to embed optional third party modules. This special feature provides extended functionality in terms of data visualisation, logic, and input processing, which only with the plain HTML standards would not be possible. There are several video and slides players used within the present Ilias installation allowing playback of embedded video and PDF files and their eventual synchronization. Separate embedded components are in fact often smaller rich internet applications.

The disadvantage of using the embedding approach is primarily that the content often can not be easily imported through the standard Ilias interface, but it requires the direct file access and advanced programming skills and experience of the course maintainer.

Generally, there are three major user roles: course participants, and content and system administrators. Course participants can access the course materials and post messages in the forums, content administrators are allowed to create and modify the content, and finally system administrators can modify and create user accounts.

All Ilias users are equipped with computers with network connection and a web browser of recent version, which is the only required equipment. The general advantage of the used thin client concept is that there is no explicit maintenance required on the client side since the workstation has to be equipped only with standard software.

Ilias includes a broad functionality for course maintenance and also incorporates the Sharable Content Object Reference Model (SCORM) for standardized import and export of content. The SCORM represents a collection of standards and specifications for e-learning systems. Its current version is SCORM 2004.

After a successful login, the system displays a 'personal desktop' (figure 4.1), where every user can customize own entry page with preferred courses. Each course consists of a set of virtual folders corresponding with separate lessons or key topics. Each folder then contains a video, downloadable slides, and an audio file with the actual learning content. Optionally also, a test generator where every participant can generate, pass through, and review an automatically prepared test, randomly generated from a pool of questions of various types.

Ilias also includes a communication framework which offers a messaging system based on the IRC protocol [56] for instant mutual communication of multiple participants in virtual rooms, forums where public communication among participants takes place, remotely resembling email conversation. The forum communication is organized in threads and each new posting is optionally propagated to the thread participants via the SMTP to their external email addresses.

The communication framework is essential for feedback facilitation between the participants and the administrators. The communication channels help to point out eventual content inconsistencies and to explain and clarify problems. All messages in forums are accessible to all course participants in order to avoid duplicate postings.

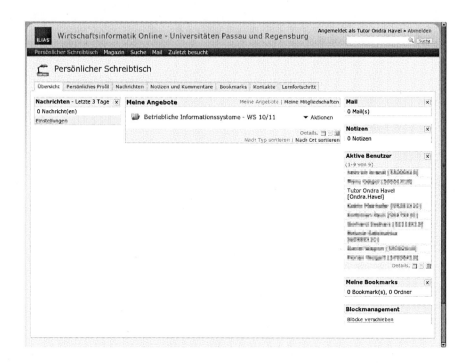

Figure 4.1: Ilias personal desktop.

The user interface is quite modern and intuitive in terms of today's standards, after only a short time an average computer literate gains feeling of orientation in the system structure. The interface is relatively simple and self-explanatory and a special training for new users is not necessary. Figure 4.2 shows an example online lecture.

4.4 Architecture

A large number of web applications in internet runs on the FOSS [88]. Thanks to the worldwide popularity, high flexibility and possibility to run almost on any hardware, the Linux platform is often chosen as the base for operating environment together with the Apache web server with PHP extensions for the dynamic web content generation. Because all used components are truly open source and they are used typically in this configuration, this combination is called briefly the LAMP architecture (Linux, Apache, MySQL, and PHP). In reality, the abbreviation 'LAMP' describes any low-cost open source architecture that relies on an

46

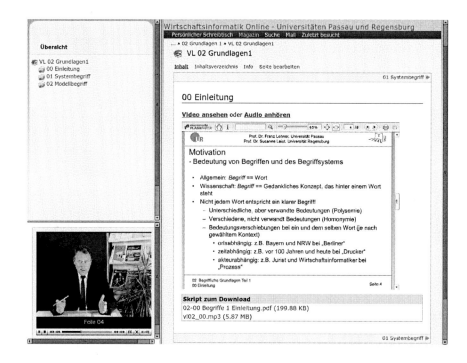

Figure 4.2: Ilias displaying a lecture.

open source operating system, open source web server, open source database, and open source programming language for its implementation, as stated by Isaias et al. [35]. For each component there are several other free alternatives.

Figure 4.3 shows a typical organization of components in a LAMP configuration. The underlying operating system runs an application server which consists of a web server with PHP extensions and a running database. The web server and the database are typically running as two concurrent processes. The web server expects incoming connections from the network, the database expects connections from the PHP application via a local TCP/IP connection. LAMP systems also combine several heterogeneous components. For performance analysis of the whole system is the utilization measurement of single components a good starting point.

4.4.1 Generic System Utilization

The most essential hardware part of a computer system is its central processing unit (CPU). Utilization is a specific factor that refers to the amount of time which

47

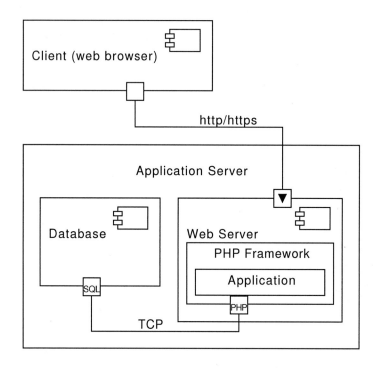

Figure 4.3: Typical LAMP architecture.

has to be provided to other system components in order to process their requests. Utilization is a percentage value that can be for any given time interval computed as a ratio of durations of idle and busy periods.

The rate of utilization provides only internal description and does not provide an external view of the component. However, the external observation can be necessary for performance estimation and analysis of the whole system. Each component can be in a broader context seen as a processing unit with associated waiting queue of incoming requests (figure 4.4). The arrival rate of incoming requests is specified by λ, the processing rate of the system component by μ.

Obviously, whenever $\lambda > \mu$, the arrival queue grows. This situation is over a long time period undesirable because the queue usually consumes system resources and its increasing length results in growing waiting times. On Windows systems, the run queue length can be observed with the Performance Monitor (perfmon) as the 'Processor Queue Length'. On Unix systems, the length of the same queue can be displayed with the vmstat command. Unix systems, however, include perhaps a slightly more sophisticated method of measuring the

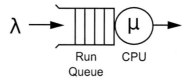

Figure 4.4: Process run queue.

run queue length and utilization with a single value.

4.4.2 Average System Load

Average system load refers to the load average values which can be specially on Unix systems displayed with the `uptime` command. It is a number showing how much work the CPU performs. Average values represent system load over a period of time, typically displayed in one-, five-, and fifteen-minute period. An idle CPU has the load number of 0 and each process using or waiting (in the run queue) for the CPU increments the value by 1. At one moment, single CPU can run only one process.

The following example [79] shows an interpretation of the `uptime` command's output '1.73 0.50 7.98' on a single-CPU system:

- during the last minute, the CPU was overloaded by 73% (1 CPU with 1.73 runnable processes, so that 0.73 processes had to wait for a turn)

- during the last 5 minutes, the CPU was underloaded 50% (no processes had to wait for a turn)

- during the last 15 minutes, the CPU was overloaded 698% (1 CPU with 7.98 runnable processes, so that 6.98 processes had to wait for a turn)

4.5 Evaluation

This chapter describes several issues which were identified in evaluations during the past years. After each semester an electronic course evaluation takes place. Course participants can express their opinions and write comments regarding the past course. This evaluation takes into account more aspects including the teachers, the learning content, and optionally also the learning platform. During the past four years (2008-20012) various and mostly recent versions of Ilias were used.

The evaluations and also the direct feedback from participants and course tutors repeatedly pointed out several common problems. The individual problems were grouped into multiple classes and they are discussed in the following chapters.

4.5.1 High Heterogeneity

One of the most often mentioned issues by the participants is the lengthy communication with course tutors. Course tutors observed and reported a similar problem independently. The problem can be more generally specified as a higher heterogeneity arising from spacial separation of the content and forum components within the Ilias system.

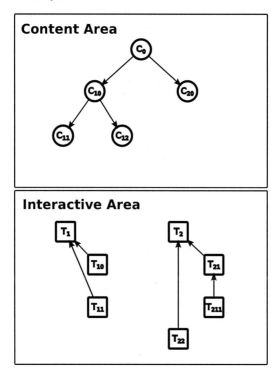

Figure 4.5: Ilias arrangement model.

For this case, the evaluations repeat similar stories:

- A participant is working with a video or slides and requires further clarification, or notices a content discrepancy and wants to notify the course maintainer about this.

- Similar situation can occur during or after a test, where a particular question might be unclear or contains an erroneous statement which the user wants to report.

In the present Ilias environment, the participant has to locate the correct communication channel, where the message could be posted. There are several forums for posting messages. The right forum has to be found and opened, consequently the message can be formulated and sent.

In order to avoid loosing the currently opened document, an additional browser window or a tab pane can be opened and the problem solved there. Albeit this flexibility can be seen as a general advantage of thin client web applications, an experiment has shown that some users tend to solve the problem only within one browser window. In this case, the original document is left and the context is lost. The context is represented by the current playing time position in a video or by the current page number. After the message was posted, the users either use the browser back button multiple times in order to return to the original page with the content or they look up the content page again and open it in the usual way. Both approaches generate multiple requests and restore a state that was already present in the past which generates additional server load.

Whenever a new message is posted, the course administrators are informed via email so that they can respond almost instantly. Similarly, the main issue reported by the administrators was that the posting often does not contain the exact location of the problematic content within the course. This often results in a lengthy conversation between the participants and the administrators which require further and precise spatial information. This negotiation apparently does not represent any benefit for other users but dwells in the system and pollutes it with its irrelevance and makes the particular forum thread uninteresting for other readers.

The coordinate system for describing the content or even particular content parts is for most users ambiguous. Some users simply can not or completely forget to add the exact spatial description.

4.5.2 Test Generator

In various past versions of Ilias the generator produces a test with multiple randomly selected questions from a question pool. This selection is saved individually for each user in the database for later use and reviews.

During the processing phase, only single questions are displayed. According to the evaluation, this is seen negatively with a proposal that it would be ideal if the representation of the test could look like a normal printed test exam containing multiple questions per page. Some participants prefer answering questions in a custom order of preference.

A usual paper version contains multiple questions on one page an allows fast non-sequential processing of the questions. If the user wants to answer the test questions in a custom order of preference, he/she can switch to the next or the previous question. Each mouse click results in an HTTP transaction which causes delays and the user has to wait. The latency is significant during the times of a higher server load and it can take several tens of seconds only to display every question in the test. However, there is yet no comfortable workaround or a patch for displaying multiple different questions on one screen for Ilias.

4.5.3 High Latency

As of the current date and configuration, approx. 50 MB of RAM are needed for one active online user in the Ilias system. During the semester, there are usually up to 150 users online simultaneously causing an enormous server load. This load increase has a significant impact on the response time. The response time can be measured as the elapsed time needed for a state change of a web application typically after a mouse click resulting in a page redraw in the browser. With a very low server load, the response varies time between 100 and 300 milliseconds. However, in a critical time period – regularly a few days before the exam – the number of online users grows significantly often causing an extreme overload.

Unfortunately, the number of online users influences the server load with multiplicative effect and also correlates with the response time. The response time on a server with a Pentium E5540 and 4 GB RAM grew up to 8 seconds, which makes the work with the system minimally very lengthy and uncomfortable. A load measurement with the real students is shown in figure 4.6. The server is remotely monitored with Nagios [36] which was also used for the generation of the chart showing the weighted moving average of the actual system load in past 1, 5, and 15 minutes.

High system load is generally an unappreciated phenomenon which negatively influences all other services running on the system. The database represents one of the central processes of information systems with a similar architecture. Overloaded host system forces the database process to stay longer in the process run queue. This additional delay influences all other processes communicating with the database. As a result, the page load times are consecutively lengthened. Overloaded host system also exhibits further purely technical side effects like excessive thermal emissions and higher power consumption.

According to the queueing theory for the overall system stability it remains essentially important that the incoming request rate remains steadily lower than

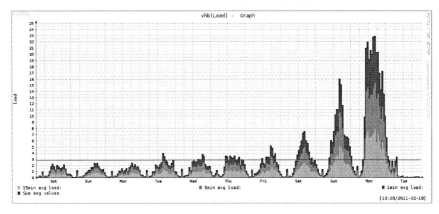

Figure 4.6: Excessive system load with 150 participants.

the processing rate [28]. Otherwise, the waiting queue can grow to an unaccept-able length and the users have to wait for their replies for a noticeably longer time. Curiously, longer waiting also discourages impatient participants from fur-ther using the system and represent an interesting auto-regulatory effect.

However, further increase of pending requests can also exhaust another op-erating system resources such as memory. This situation is strongly undesirable under some operating systems. Linux kernels, for instance, terminate some of the running processes in order to make at least some memory available. If either the database or the web server processes are terminated, the system stops functioning properly and it requires an intervention of the administrator.

In order to provide enough memory for the worst-case scenario for 1000 ac-tive clients, approx. 48 GB of operating memory would have to be installed. The system load would be accordingly high and with recent hardware, the mean response time could be yet acceptable. Although such hardware configuration would be today already affordable, such upscaling is certainly not the only way for improving the performance.

Figure 4.7 shows the increasing CPU load with the increasing number of active sessions in two separated charts. An active session represents a participant which has performed at least one HTTP request within the last minute. The charts show an overloaded system during a different course on a slightly newer hardware with a Xeon E5649 and 8 GB of RAM but with only 60 parallel sessions.

53

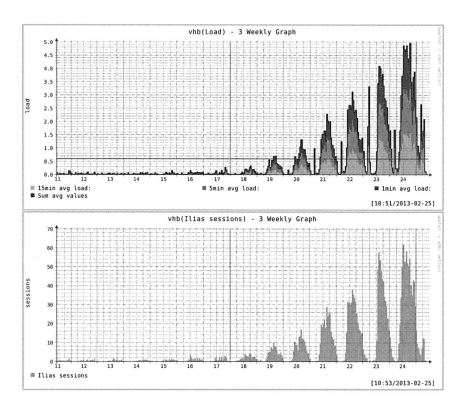

Figure 4.7: Ilias load with the number of sessions.

4.5.4 Low Availability

With an insufficient hardware configuration the system's region of acceptance could became too narrow for a higher amount of incoming connections. Because under the used configuration, there exists a fixed memory/participant ratio, the task to predict the critical time when the whole system could collapse is fairly simple.

Sufficient amount of operating memory is the mandatory condition for the long term system stability. As can be clearly seen in figures 4.7 and 4.6, the amount of connections reaches to its maximum a few days before the final exam. For obvious reasons, it is also very unpleasant if the server collapses just during that time.

4.6 Summary

The Ilias learning management system includes a variety of functions which can be combined in order to create a suitable environment almost for any required configuration. Albeit the configuration possibilities are certainly broad, even simply configured, the system does not provide enough performance for hundreds of users. The performance drops further with the growing amount of simultaneous connections which is accompanied by a heavy server load.

A heavy server load is a generally unappreciated phenomenon which causes excessive power consumption and heat dissipation on the currently used hardware. The varying temperature and the high frequency of temperature changes can lead to a faster material wear and result in hardware specific problems. For participants, the higher server load is represented by longer waiting times. Conducted measurements suggest that the high consumption of the system time is probably caused by the suboptimal arrangement of the internal elements within the software system.

Using suitable technologies, it seems that the server load could be reduced by moving and running selected parts of its logic at the client side. The presence of logic at the client side can also be utilized in several ways, for instance, for reducing of the communication flow between the server and the client. How significant and demanding this change could be and could the performance of a new system developed using this concept be simply 'good enough'? Theoretically, present hardware should be able to provide services with a better performance with ease, but so far there seem to be no alternatives available that would be able to clearly outperform Ilias. Answer to these open questions will also be found empirically by creation of a new alternative system and its testing with the real users.

Chapter 5

New Prototype Framework

This chapter introduces the design and development of a completely new web e-learning system. The system utilizes a generic framework implemented using the rich internet application concept utilizing session connections. This arrangement should provide a more comfortable user interface and it also should result in an improved overall system performance in comparison to the standard thin client web applications and especially Ilias.

5.1 Introduction

Ilias in a configuration that has been used during the past online courses was used as the reference system. The newly developed prototype should result in a working system which can fully substitute Ilias. Additionally, the disadvantages identified in the evaluations were also kept in mind and the prototype tries to avoid them.

The following chapters describe also selected considerations and measurements that preceded the implementation, the internal system structure, and its basic mechanisms. First, the functional specification describing the basic framework is outlined and its main subsystems and interfaces are identified. Several possible alternatives are considered for every data transport and data storage, and the most suitable methods are preferred according to the results of comparison measurements.

5.2 Functional Specification

This chapter describes the abstract mechanisms for rudimentary data interchange at the lowest level primarily between the users and the server. The introduced transport model is required to identify and fulfill the typical tasks in an e-learning system. The prototype utilizes this model and the described mechanisms create the vital part of the software.

The global system includes at least one central courseware server and all of its connected clients. Every client may join or leave the system at any time. The rate of this activity is called the volatility. System components with high volatility are marked with a dot.

Elementary unit that is used for data interchange among various subsystems is called the event. Events are created and propagated in order to spread a new information quickly in the system.

The following system definition is completely formal. It presents the system as a specific set of function blocks and interfaces.

$$S = \left(\dot{E}, \dot{R}, \dot{A}, T \right)$$

The key components are:

- $\dot{E}$ – The set of event generators (emitters) providing information which should be spread in the system. For instance, upload of a new file or a new posting in a discussion forum are examples of event generators.

- $\dot{R}$ – The set of event consumers (receptors) obtaining and processing information which is typically either displayed or stored in the database and kept persistent. A client receiving notification about a newly uploaded file is a possible example of an event consumer.

- $\dot{A}$ – Transformation $\dot{A} : \dot{R}_i \rightarrow \dot{E}$ describes which consumers receive information from which emitters. A general role-based access control (RBAC) facility, content mirroring, but also other miscellaneous tasks like chat rooms of the instant messaging component are implemented as specializations of this transformation.

- T – The set of transport subsystems:

$$T_s(\dot{E}_i, \dot{R}_j)$$
$$T_s \subset T, \dot{E}_i \subset \dot{E}, \dot{R}_j \subset \dot{R}$$

T is typically used for data interchange on the network level but also within multithreaded and concurrent processing environments. The network transport includes the TCP/IP connection, the HTTP protocol, and the session connection with a custom application protocol. The communication among threads and processes involves the use of specialized libraries.

Primary tasks of the system S are:

- Keeping the information contained within S always consistent.

- Immediate parameter correction of relevant subsystems after each state change initiated by an event generation.

- $\forall \dot{R}_i \ Load(T(A(\dot{R}_i), \dot{R}_i)) \rightarrow min$

  Minimization of the load caused by the transportation to the host system.

- $\forall \dot{E}_i \ Load(\dot{E}_i) \rightarrow min, \forall \dot{R}_i \ Load(\dot{R}_i) \rightarrow min$

  Minimization of the load of the host systems of all receptors and all emitters.

5.3   Architecture

The basic functionality and requirements on each component were described very formally. The problem is now to find and implement an appropriate combination of components which will work together conforming to the requirements of the functional specification. However, the target is not to achieve full compliance and implement everything from scratch, but to make use of existing standards, libraries, and ready-made components, in order to reduce the programming effort and required time. This standpoint also influenced the selection of programming language chosen for the server.

Some of the alternative technologies were already introduced in the initial chapter. The client application was implemented as a RIA. RIA allows to run its own logic on the client with support of additional session connections. With this vision in mind, the basic architecture with elementary building blocks can be outlined in figure 5.1.

Initial concern that *"a predominate number of negative issues that should be understood before making the decision to embrace the use of free open source software"* as stated by Schmidt et al. [66] was not confirmed.

The proposal of a suitable partitioning of a web application between the server and the client by Kuuskeri et al. [42] seems right and it can simplify the parallel development of both client and server applications. Although the server and the client were written in completely different programming languages, the assumption that a complex client/server solution *"should be built using fewer technologies and a single programming language"* as stated in the same source was rejected. Data structure compatibility and reciprocal serialization methods in both client and server were the key point for a comfortable implementation on both ends.

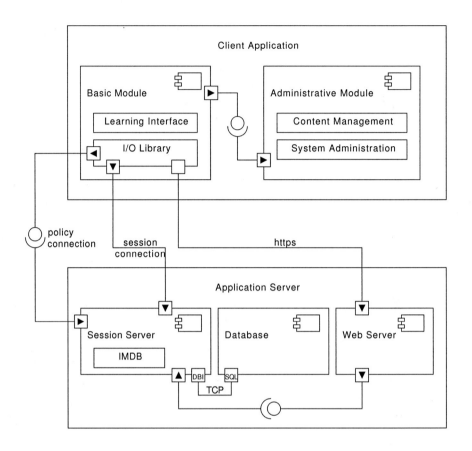

Figure 5.1: Architecture diagram of the client/server setup.

Frameworks like Banzai [13] provide a similar functionality for high performance servers with a simple architecture. However, the asynchronous channel in this solution is based on a lower level protocol and completely different programming languages.

Gutwin et al. [32] provide an exhausting survey of methods for implementation of the session connection channel stating that the *"recent advances in web-based networking open the door to supporting real-time interaction in plain browser"* which is very promising with respect to future versions of the prototype.

Nicula [51] proposes an implementation based on clients running Flash and communicating through an XML socket which is a popular approach that was used originally in the first version of the prototype and it also worked very well, but in order to avoid computational penalty caused by reciprocal XML conversions and parsing, the AMF3 based protocol has proven itself as a quicker and simpler solution in the current implementation.

Sources of latency in a system utilizing only a plain HTTP connection are well described in a preliminary evaluation by [57] Popa et al.

5.4 Development Process

Contrary to the linear software development model as proposed by Schäfer [65], the spiral model by Boehm [7] (figure 5.2) was used during the creation of the prototype. Agarwal et al. [1] state that the spiral model is an evolutionary model that couples the iterative nature of prototyping with the controlled systematic aspects of the linear segmented model.

The iterative approach of the spiral model was very beneficial during the initial development phases of the client application. One of the essential tasks was to find a suitable user interface framework. There are several implementations of graphical user interfaces (GUI) for Flex publicly available. The spiral model enabled to combine the user interface evaluation with the code development and in every verification phase the GUI could be eventually replaced with a better implementation.

The Flex framework itself was developed simultaneously. Flex 3 was actively developed during 2008 to 2011, Flex 4 then since 2010. The iterative approach allowed to evaluate new features of the latest Flex framework and their incorporation in the prototype. Smooth transition from Flex 3 to Flex 4 was performed as well. Initially, commercial Adobe Flash Builder[1] was used as integrated development environment, recent versions require exclusively open source tools for compilation.

Although only long-term stable modules were used during the development of the server, the spiral model manifested its benefit also in this area. On the one hand, the development cycles were partly synchronized with the development of the client, on the other hand, the iterative approach allowed to test alternative technologies specific for the server.

5.5 Reference System

The hardware configuration used during the creation of this work consists of an ordinary notebook computer with Intel i3-2367M CPU, 8 GB operating memory, and one gigabit Ethernet network connection. The hardware runs open

---

[1]Adobe Flash Builder (previously known as Adobe Flex Builder) is an integrated development environment built on the Eclipse platform.

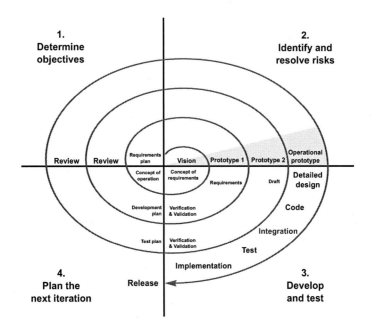

1.
Determine
objectives

2.
Identify and
resolve risks

Review | Review | Requirements plan | Vision | Prototype 1 | Prototype 2 | Operational prototype

Concept of operation | Concept of requirements | Requirements | Draft | Detailed design

Development plan | Verification & Validation | Code

Integration

Test plan | Verification & Validation | Test

Implementation

4.
Plan the
next iteration

Release

3.
Develop
and test

Figure 5.2: Spiral model.

source software on a recent version (12.04) of Ubuntu Linux distribution. Unless specified otherwise, all of the tests and benchmarks performed were conducted with this configuration. The memory bus has 64 bit data length and there are two SODIMM-factor DDR3-type memory modules installed and clocked at 1333 MHz. Listing 5.1 shows a more detailed information regarding the CPU.

Listing 5.1: Output of the lscpu command.

```
Architecture:          x86_64
CPU op-mode(s):        32-bit, 64-bit
Byte Order:            Little Endian
CPU(s):                4
On-line CPU(s) list:   0-3
Thread(s) per core:    2
Core(s) per socket:    2
Socket(s):             1
NUMA node(s):          1
Vendor ID:             GenuineIntel
CPU family:            6
Model:                 42
Stepping:              7
CPU MHz:               1400.000
BogoMIPS:              2793.54
```

```
Virtualization:        VT-x
L1d cache:             32K
L1i cache:             32K
L2 cache:              256K
L3 cache:              3072K
NUMA node0 CPU(s):     0-3
```

5.6   Programming Environment

The initial versions of the prototype were implemented with Perl and Flex. Perl excels at rapid application development and there is a large amount of modules for almost any task publicly available. The Flex framework provides a universal operating environment within most web browsers and it is able to communicate with Perl applications without problems.

5.6.1   Perl Data Types

According to the sophisticated documentation of Perl [14], the language has three built-in data types: scalars, arrays of scalars, and associative arrays of scalars known as 'hashes'. A scalar is a single string of any size (limited only by the available memory), a number, or a reference to some other variable. Normal arrays are ordered lists of scalars indexed by a number, starting with zero. Hashes are unordered collections of scalar values indexed by their associated string key.

Scalar values are always named with '$', even when referring to a scalar that is part of an array or a hash. The '$' symbol works semantically like the English word 'the' in that it indicates a single value is expected.

```
$days               # the simple scalar value "days"
$days[28]           # the 29th element of array @days
$days{'Feb'}        # the 'Feb' value from hash %days
```

Entire arrays (and slices of arrays and hashes) are denoted by '@', which works much as the word 'these' or 'those' does in English, in that it indicates multiple values are expected.

```
@days               # ($days[0], $days[1],... $days[n])
@days[3,4,5]        # same as ($days[3],$days[4],$days[5])
@days{'a','c'}      # same as ($days{'a'},$days{'c'})
```

Entire hashes are denoted by '%':

63

```
%days              # (key1, val1, key2, val2 ...)
```

A reference to an existing variable can be created by using the backslash operator or directly by an assignment with a specific syntax.

```
$arefdays = \@days;
$aref = [1, 2, 3];   # array reference
$href = {k => 'a'};  # hash reference
```

A reference variable can be dereferenced by using the '$' or the '->' operators.

```
$$arefdays[0]        # same as $days[0]
$arefdays->[0]       # same as $days[0]
```

5.6.2   ActionScript Data Types

Contrary to Perl, a single variable in ActionScript 3.0 can utilize one of the following data types: String, Boolean, Number, integer (int), and unsigned integer (uint). In order to work with complex data structures, Array and Object types are needed. They are counterparts to arrays and hashes in Perl. ActionScript works with a slightly different syntax which was originally derived from ECMAScript[2] [48].

```
var array : Array = [ 1, 2, 3 ];
var hash  : Object = { key0: "Value0", key1: 1 };
```

5.7   Data Interchange Methods

Transformation of computer program data into a suitable form which can be stored or transmitted is called the serialization. The opposite process, when serialized data are transformed back into its original outgoing format is called the deserialization. Serialization libraries typically include both transformation processes. Most programming languages support data serialization either directly with a built-in implementation or indirectly using an additional library. A suitable serialization is often also the only way for data interchange within a heterogeneous system.

---

[2]ECMAScript is the scripting language standardized by Ecma International in the ECMA-262 specification and ISO/IEC 16262.

The following chapters offer a short look at some universal and established serialization techniques which work reliable and are commonly used in the heterogeneous environments. Focus was given on the time required for the transformation in Perl and on the output data sizes. The origin of the tested methods is various. Some of them produce a compact binary output and they were originally developed and used for the data interchange of telecommunication devices, other were primarily developed for the data interchange within software systems. However, they all fulfill the same purpose and make communication within a heterogeneous system possible. Methods in table 5.3 are listed in alphabetical order of their respective names.

Name	Norm	Binary	HR[a]
AMF 3	AMF 3 Specification	Yes	No
ASN.1	ITU-T X.680	Yes (BER[b], PER[c])	Yes (XER[d])
XML	W3C	No	Yes
JSON	RFC 4672	No	Yes

[a]human readable
[b]Basic Encoding Rules
[c]Packed Encoding Rules
[d]XML Encoding Rules

Figure 5.3: Short summary of selected serialization methods.

There were several different data types used for the measurements, combining binary and text, from plain structures to more complex hierarchical structures. This should have helped to identify the most suitable method for the implementation. As a simple example, following short input (listing 5.2) was also used and serialized. Separate chapters regarding each method contain a listing of the respective output.

Listing 5.2: Example serialization input.

```
$object = {
    string => 'Quick brown fox jumps over the lazy dog.',
    array  => [ 1, 1.61803398875 ],
    hash   => { key0 => 'a', key1 => [ 'b', 'c' ] },
};
```

Action Message Format

Action Message Format in version 3 (AMF3) is a binary data format originally developed by Macromedia for data interchange between Flash clients and the Flash Media Server. The protocol specification was first published on December 13,

2007 by Adobe Systems [80]. The predecessor version of AMF3 was called AMF0 which offered a slightly reduced amount of supported data types in comparison to AMF3.

Listing 5.3: AMF3 serialization output (hexadecimal dump).

```
00  0a 0b 01 09 68 61 73 68  0a 01 09 6b 65 79 31 09   |....hash...key1.|
10  05 01 06 03 62 06 03 63  09 6b 65 79 30 06 03 61   |....b..c.key0..a|
20  01 0b 61 72 72 61 79 09  05 01 04 01 05 3f f9 e3   |..array......?..|
30  77 9b 97 f6 82 0d 73 74  72 69 6e 67 06 51 51 75   |w.....string.QQu|
40  69 63 6b 20 62 72 6f 77  6e 20 66 6f 78 20 6a 75   |ick brown fox ju|
50  6d 70 73 20 6f 76 65 72  20 74 68 65 20 6c 61 7a   |mps over the laz|
60  79 20 64 6f 67 2e 01                               |y dog..|
67
```

The AMF3 method works very similarly to ASN.1. The major advantage over ASN.1 is the ability of ad hoc processing of arbitrary data structures. Albeit AMF3 makes use of a special format for representing integers with the mechanism for reducing the required space, this method is not as flexible as the one in ASN.1 and the major disadvantage is just the integer interpretation used for description of lengths of individual record entities with its maximal value limited to $2^{29} - 1$.

Abstract Syntax Notation One

Abstract Syntax Notation One (ASN.1) is a very universal notation for describing of complex data structures including their encoding, transmission, and decoding in computer networks and telecommunication infrastructures. ASN.1 itself was created as a joint standard of the International Organization for Standardization (ISO) already in 1984 and it is often used as a communication tool within a heterogeneous systems. Dubuisson [20] describes the whole standard with a variety of encoding rules in detail.

Unlike other serialization methods, the data structure has to be described in advance before the transformation using a special syntax. Listing 5.4 shows a record that was used for transformation of the example input.

Listing 5.4: ASN.1 input structure description.

```
[APPLICATION 7] SEQUENCE {
    string OCTET STRING,
    array SEQUENCE OF REAL,
    hash SET {
        key0 OCTET STRING,
        key1 SEQUENCE OF OCTET STRING
    }
}
```

Listing 5.5 shows that the ASN.1 serialization produces the shortest output from the example input data. However, a look in more detail reveals that the

66

hash key names were completely omitted which results in shorter outputs, but renders the method unsuitable for ad hoc data serialization of arbitrary data structures.

Listing 5.5: ASN.1 serialization output (BER hexadecimal dump).

```
00   67 49 04 28 51 75 69 63   6b 20 62 72 6f 77 6e 20   |gI.(Quick brown |
10   66 6f 78 20 6a 75 6d 70   73 20 6f 76 65 72 20 74   |fox jumps over t|
20   68 65 20 6c 61 7a 79 20   64 6f 67 2e 30 10 09 03   |he lazy dog.0...|
30   80 f9 80 09 09 80 c9 cf   1b bc dc bf b4 10 31 0b   |..............1.|
40   04 01 61 30 06 04 01 62   04 01 63               |..a0...b..c|
4b
```

The BER serialization output in listing 5.5 uses a system of prefixes to describe data types, lengths, and contents of all processed values. For example, the initial $0x67$ determines the type of the main structure and the $0x49$ is its length, also 73 bytes. Similarly, the next byte, $0x04$ determines the string type and the $0x28$ (40 decimal) the length of the 'Quick brown fox...' string. The output is also byte aligned. In order to achieve yet more compact output, the packed encoding rules can be used. The outstanding feature of ASN.1 is its universality which consists in the possibility to work with arbitrarily long integers. Because integers are used for length descriptions, the ASN.1 is also able to process arbitrarily long data records.

Extensible Markup Language

The special feature of the Extensible Markup Language (XML) is its specific output format. Data encoded with XML are both machine- and human-readable. The benefit of this feature is its great overall simplicity and generality in a host of applications.

Listing 5.6: XML serialization output.

```
<perldata>
 <hashref memory_address="0x10eee68">
  <item key="array">
   <arrayref memory_address="0x10d1998">
    <item key="0">1</item>
    <item key="1">1.61803398875</item>
   </arrayref>
  </item>
  <item key="hash">
   <hashref memory_address="0x10eee80">
    <item key="key0">a</item>
    <item key="key1">
     <arrayref memory_address="0x10eed60">
      <item key="0">b</item>
      <item key="1">c</item>
     </arrayref>
    </item>
   </hashref>
  </item>
```

67

```
<item key="string">Quick brown fox jumps over the lazy dog.</item>
</hashref>
</perldata>
```

XML is able to work with arbitrarily long data records as well as ASN.1. The serialized output of individual records does not implicitly contain the length information. On the other hand, handling of special characters, which can be used directly in the content but could also be used for building of the tag structure, is required. This procedure is called escaping and denotes a substitution of control characters with a special string.

"	&quot;
'	&apos;
<	&lt;
>	&gt;
&	&amp;

Figure 5.4: XML escape sequences.

Although there are only five escape sequences (table 5.4), all input characters have to be checked and eventually translated.

JavaScript Object Notation

The JavaScript Object Notation (JSON) is another text-based open standard for specific data interchange purposes. The typical use of JSON is data serialization, transmission, and deserialization. Unlike XML, the JSON specification is much simpler.

Listing 5.7: JSON serialization output (116 bytes).

```
{
  "hash":{
          "key1":["b","c"],
          "key0":"a"
          },
  "array":[1,1.61803398875],
  "string":"Quick brown fox jumps over the lazy dog."
}
```

Albeit JSON is sometimes called the fat-free alternative to XML, the method also has to deal with the escaping of characters. One of the advantages over XML is the shorter output, but on the other hand, the readability for humans is not as good. Listing 5.7 contains an additional whitespace for better readability.

Serialization Benchmarks

This chapter takes a closer look at some results using various data serialization methods implemented in Perl. For Perl, there is a large online archive of modules available called the Comprehensive Perl Archive Network (CPAN). The CPAN contains over 120000 modules [83]. Some popular CPAN modules are often standardly available and installable as ordinary operating system packages. Otherwise, a custom package can be downloaded directly from the CPAN, compiled, tested, and installed.

The comparison was conducted with formerly introduced methods (AMF3, XML, JSON)[3] . ASN.1 was omitted, because it is not suitable for ad hoc serialization of completely generic structures. Instead, Perl Storable, a native module for data serialization in Perl environments was chosen for the comparison. The comparison was conducted with multiple different sets of data with varying length, type, and hierarchical complexity. The results show the output size and the total time which was needed to process the data, the shorter is the better. There are many different implementations in many programming languages with varying efficiency, so this overview describes the performance of individual Perl modules rather than the serialization methods themselves. However, the specification of each serialization method has an impact on the performance of each respective implementation.

- Processing of a short array containing one short scalar element.

  Slightly higher amount of required CPU time can be observed by the XML method. XML also generates the longest output.

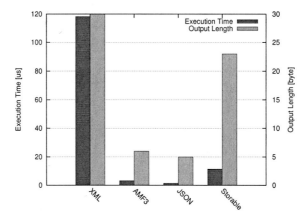

Figure 5.5: *Measurements with a short array.*

---

[3]Storable::AMF3, JSON, and XML::Simple modules were used.

- Processing of an array with 1024 short scalars.

  This measurement shows a higher CPU needed to process the data with the XML method.

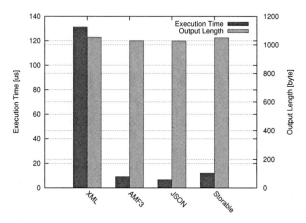

Figure 5.6: *Measurements with an array with 1024 short scalars.*

- Processing of a hash with scalar values.

  Surprisingly, the JSON method consumes a lot of CPU time and produces the longest output in comparison to other methods.

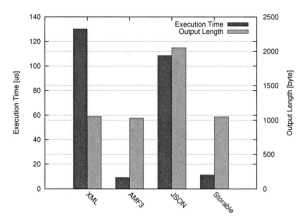

Figure 5.7: *Measurements with a hash with scalar values.*

- Processing of a complex hierarchical data structure including a hash with nested array references with binary data.

Although the JSON module performs slightly faster than the AMF3 module, its output is the longest one.

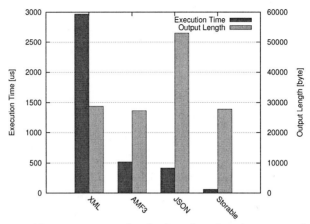

Figure 5.8: *Measurements with a hash with scalar elements with binary data.*

- Processing of a complex hierarchical data structure including a hash with nested array references.

  It seems that the JSON module performs very well as long as it has not to deal with binary data. In JSON, binary data is escaped, producing a significantly longer output.

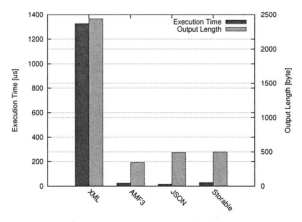

Figure 5.9: *Measurements with a complex hierarchical structure.*

- Time comparison with the deserialization process.

  With XML, it can be clearly seen that the deserialization process is almost as CPU time intensive as the serialization. During the deserialization, the whole XML structure has to be analyzed and syntactically checked. First after a successful check, the data can be extracted. Compared to other methods, the CPU time penalty of XML deserialization seems to be enormous.

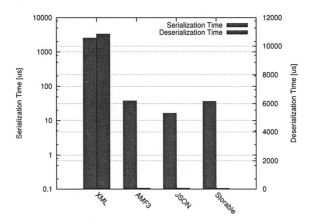

Figure 5.10: *Measurements of both processes.*

Suitable Methods

It seems that XML and AMF3 are the most suitable candidates for the serialization channel between Perl and ActionScript, since in ActionScript there is a native support for both formats. The performance measurements show that the server needs much less time for processing the AMF3 data and produces shorter outputs, especially while working with structures containing binary data.

The AMF3 binary format is also used for data interchange between the server and clients. On the client, there is native support available in the standard Flex libraries for encoding and decoding of AMF3. On the server, a very fast Storable::AMF3 [26] or less powerful Data::AMF [50] modules can be used.

Initial prototype versions used serialized XML structures mainly for debug reasons. Outstanding performance and mutual data structure compatibility of the AMF3 parsers on both sides decided clearly in favour of AMF3. AMF3 offers more feasible implementation with respect to serialized output length, error checking during the deserialization, and variety of supported data formats. The original XML interchange support was dropped completely in recent versions.

5.8 Server

The server is intended to run in a Unix environment as a compound product consisting of a web server with CGI support, an SQL database, and a session server. The Apache [24] and thttpd [63] have proven to work very well in such configuration. As database, PostgreSQL 8.4 [73] is used. For the SQL database access, the standard DBI module is used as described by [39] Kleinschmidt et al.

The running of a rich internet application is more complicated compared to the thin client architecture. First, the client application downloads the application binary from the web server via the HTTP protocol. The binary is embedded in an HTML page. The HTML page also contains a complete configuration record for the embedded application. This record describes all TCP addresses of the cloud servers.

After a successful download and execution within the Flash Player, the application in order to open a session connection requests the crossdomain.xml file with the remote access policy specification. This is a plain text file and it is also hosted by the web server. The client requests and performs authentication and transmits user credentials via HTTPS to the web server. This encrypted connection is fully handled and its secureness indicated by the browser in a usual manner. Most browsers show a symbol in the address bar indicating that the connection is encrypted an also provide complete certificate information upon request.

Secureness during the login process is mandatory because the authentication is performed against third-party systems at the university and the credential information must not be transmitted in plain text in any case. The web part of the solution performs authentication and passes its result further to the main process through a local socket. Presently, there is no encryption used within the persistent session connection. However, there is a possibility to secure the session connection with encryption using the AS3 Crypto library [53]. Unfortunately, there is no native mechanism for checking and indicating the connection secureness status within Flash so far. There is also no suitable possibility to display the certificate chain. For this reason, the HTTPS is used for critical operations like authentications and password manipulations.

After a successful authentication the client and server communicate mostly by exchanging events through the persistent session socket. Implementations of various multimedia player libraries assume often the HTTP as the only transport protocol for the network resource access. For this reason, the multimedia files like videos and slides are distributed through the web server. The existence of the separate session and HTTP connections resembles the pair of separate signaling and data connections in voice over IP (VoIP) networks [38] but primarily provides the security benefit of the HTTPS utilization.

5.8.1 Hardware Requirements

The hardware requirements of the prototype are minimal. The software requires a server with 128 MB of free RAM with the ability to run Perl 5.14 and a web server with CGI support. Each client connection consumes approximately 256 byte of RAM. With this requirements it should be possible to run the software even on a very weak hardware. In order to confirm this assumption, the software was successfully configured and run on a Raspberry Pi computer.

5.8.2 Running on Raspberry Pi

In late 2011 a powerful single-board computer, the Raspberry Pi, was introduced. With the list price of $35, 512 MB of operating memory, 700 Mhz ARM1176JZF-S processor represented one of the cheapest single-board computers that time. According to Wired [25], Raspberry Pi quickly approaches one million units sold. The power consumption of the computer is below 3 Watt.

The first experiments with the small computer showed that its performance could be satisfactory for running the prototype. Although not originally intended, a performance test was conducted with the older version of Raspberry with only 256 MB of RAM (figure 5.11). The test result indicates that the computer is able to handle over 100 simultaneous connections providing a reasonable performance.

5.9 Throughput of IPC Methods

The server consists of several separate processes and threads which communicate mutually. Mutual communication means synchronization and time penalty for data transmission. A short benchmark was conducted in order to show the performance differences of selected IPC methods implemented in Perl and to help indicating the most suitable method. The measurement consists in transmitting and receiving 1 GB of random data divided into fixed size packets from 2^3 to 2^{10} bytes.

The results in figure 5.12 show clearly that the shared memory access provides by far the best performance in Perl environment and it becomes the preferred communication method between server components.

5.10 Database

The most intensively used component in a typical Ilias installation is the database. Incoming queries generate high system load, the database starts to consume high

Figure 5.11: Raspberry Pi running the prototype.

amounts of the CPU time and slows down concurrently running web server processes which have to wait a longer time for results of each database query. Curioso et al. [16] suggest to perform an SQL query optimization in various ways in order to increase the overall performance but also insists that the best optimization option is to eliminate the SQL queries completely.

The analysis of the past courses has shown that the effective read/write ratio is higher than 100/1 and that the substantial amount of small data could be kept in the operating memory in order to reduce the access latency dramatically. Also with the drawing logic of the user interface and other ancillary functions moved to the client application, the amount of exchanged information was reduced substantially. If the communication with the SQL database would be prevented, the internal communication among the server threads and processes would also be reduced in a similar manner by keeping the information permanently in the operating memory. This idea is also supported by the long term sinking prices of memory media as reported by McCallum [47] in figure 5.13.

A measurement comparing several databases was conducted to find the fastest database engine. During the measurement, only elementary tasks like reading and writing were performed in order to compare a wider set of databases including noSQL engines working exclusively with plain key/value data. All information

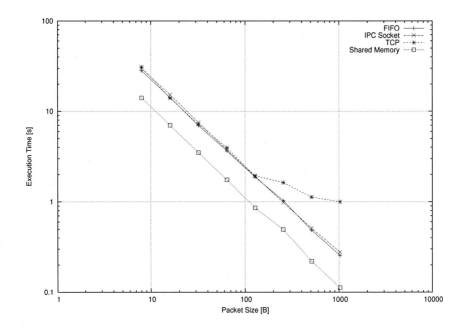

Figure 5.12: Comparison of selected IPC methods.

regarding worldwide popularity of each database was taken from solid IT [84]. For the measurement, the following database engines were used:

- **MySQL (version 5.1)**
  Worldwide mostly used open source relational database.

- **PostgreSQL (version 9.1)** is currently the second mostly used relational database worldwide.

- **BerkeleyDB (version 5.1)** is a high performance non-relational database implemented as embedded library for work with key/value data.

- **In-Memory Database** in implementation which is also used by the prototype. Chapter 5.10.1 refers to the library in more detail. This approach works with data exclusively in the operating memory and unlike previous databases does not offer a persistent data storage.

MySQL, PostgreSQL, and BerkeleyDB are delivered as standard packages in most free operating system distributions.

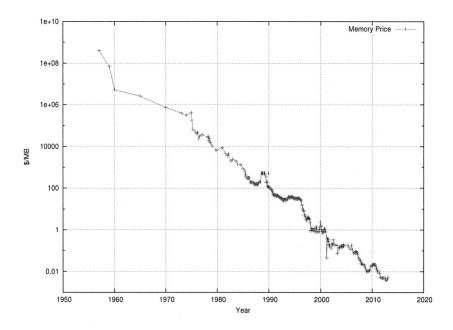

Figure 5.13: Historical cost of computer memory.

The results show the average transaction time for each operation (10^4 samples) in each database. Performed operations were: sequential write, random read, and random update. The key is represented by an integer variable, the value represents 256 bytes of a random data. During the benchmark process, the default reference configuration was used as described in chapter 5.5. The configuration files of each database were after the installation left intact, so every database was running in its default distribution specific setup.

The figure 5.14 shows only a slight difference between both SQL databases and a small performance advantage of MySQL over PostgreSQL. Note that only elementary I/O operations were performed. Substantially shorter average transaction times were achieved by both non-relational databases. The cause of the huge difference is the IPC communication performed through a local TCP/IP connection as described in chapter 3.2 and additional SQL query parsing which both require additional synchronization and CPU time. The native in-memory database (IMDB) provides an outstanding performance because it does not perform any write operations with a peripheral device unlike the Berkeley Database which accesses a file.

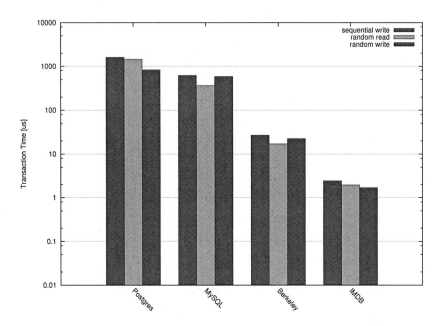

Figure 5.14: Average transaction times of selected databases.

5.10.1 In-Memory Database

This chapter provides a closer look at the specific Perl IMDB implementation and its technical details.

As can be seen in the database scheme listing 5.14 on page 82, the database structure is very simple, primary keys are present in every table. The original SQL scheme was taken apart, the complex SQL queries and views were removed and their equivalents were implemented directly within the Perl source code.

Upon server startup, the IMDB has to be initialized. The easiest possibility was to use an SQL database as the initial data source. In such case, the server loads the complete content of selected tables during the startup. The content of every table is stored in a hash variable, where each row is represented as a *key* → *row* record. Each row-value is then again mostly a hash with table attributes used as keys for accessing the data, *attribute* → *value*.

Listing 5.8: Implementation of an elementary IMDB.

```
package OLS::IO::msg;

use strict;
use warnings;
```

78

```
use OLS::IO;
use OLS::logger;

our %content;

sub load_imdb {
    OLS::IO::load_href( 'select * from messages', 'id',
           \%content );
}

sub create($$$$) {
    my ( $session, $lid, $name, $text ) = @_;

    my $sth = $dbh->prepare(
            'insert into messages (id,name,text) values(?,?,?)')
        or $session->throw('insert prepare failed')
        and return;

    my $r = $sth->execute( $lid, $name, $text )
        or $session->throw('insert failed')
        and return;

    $content{$lid} = { name => $name, text => $text };

    return 1;
}

sub remove {
    my ( $session, $id ) = @_;

    my $r = $dbh->do( 'delete from labels where id = '
            . $dbh->quote($id) )
        or $session->throw( 'delete failed' );

    delete $content{$id};

    return $r;
}

1;
```

5.10.2 SQL Persistence Layer

In order to minimize the CPU load generated at the host system, a persistent in-memory database was implemented as an integral part of the session server. The SQL database is used as a persistent storage and it is accessed only rarely, when data is modified or created. Also after a software crash or a power outage, the system resumes to the last working state during the startup by resuming the

IMDB from the SQL backup. Since the overall data amount is relatively small in respect of today's RAM chips sizes and prices, and considering that the most common operation is reading, this approach seems reasonable.

The loading of the initial database is shown in listing 5.8. First, the `load_imdb` subroutine is called by the system core. The `create` subroutine is called whenever a new entity ought to be added into the database. In this case, an ordinary SQL insert query is executed first by the backend database and on success, the new data is also written into the IMDB structure itself. This approach is quite simple but not very efficient if the amount of write requests is too high. In that case, such implementation would not offer any performance advantage over a normal SQL database. Another approach is to create a queue of SQL queries which is processed by a different thread in the background. The performance gain in this case is huge as can be seen in the presented IMDB and SQL comparison. The hybrid approach of a combined IMDB-SQL database is suitable for systems with high read/write ratio. For read accesses, the global `%content` hash variable is directly used by a special function which creates a thread-safe copy of the required entity.

5.11 Client

Actionscript 3.0 [81] was chosen as the programming language using the open source version of Apache Flex SDK[4] [82] for the complete implementation of the client. The client was also implemented as a RIA. It requires either a common web browser with installed Flash Player extension or a standalone Flash Player. The standalone player was used mostly for debugging purposes during the development. A typical intended user will be equipped with a web browser.

Although there were some drawbacks regarding the SDK which appeared during the development, the first working prototype was quite quickly implemented using the Flex framework. The implementation of the session connection library basically utilizes only the `flash.net.Socket` class and its `readObject` and `writeObject` methods. The Flex framework also allowed to implement the graphical user interface in form of a multiple document interface (MDI). An MDI gives users more flexibility at work with the application as the environment reminds in fact more of a windowing manager of an operating system rather than a web application and implements truly the model-view-controller scheme.

Minimal requirements of Adobe Flash Player 11 for desktop computers are:

- x86 compatible processor with at least 2.33 GHz (or at least 1.6 GHz for netbooks)

---

[4]Formerly Adobe Flex SDK.

- Windows XP (32 bit) or higher, or Mac OS 10.6, 10.7, or 10.8, or Linux of recent version

- Internet Explorer 7.0, Mozilla Firefox 17, Google Chrome, Safari 5.0, Opera 11

- 512 MB of RAM, 128 MB of VRAM

5.12 Data De/Serialization with AMF3

This section offers a closer look at mutual data serialization and deserialization processes in both client and server implementations. For data interchange, an ordinary TCP/IP client-to-server session connection is used and AMF3 packets are exchanged exclusively within this connection. Because the TCP lacks support of delimitation, an additional information regarding transmitted data length is required. The structure of transmitted data is shown in figure 5.15.

Figure 5.15: Data packet transmitted on the session connection.

Currently, only serialized AMF3 data units are exchanged within the session connection. As can be seen in chapter 5.7 on page 58, the AMF3 serialized data already contains the length information which also could be used directly for the delimitation purposes in the near future. Although the present generic delimitation mechanism occupies an additional space, its utilization makes an eventual substitution of the serialization mechanism quickly possible.

The following code snippet shows the mechanism for data transmission and delimitation in its ActionScript specific implementation.

Listing 5.9: Data serialization in ActionScript.

```
public function sendObject(o : Object) : void
{
    var b : ByteArray = new ByteArray();
    b.writeObject(o);
    socket.writeInt(b.length);
    socket.writeBytes(b, 0, b.length);
    socket.flush();
}
```

After receiving data from the source, the client runs the following code after a whole AMF3 packet has been received. In case of corrupted or incompatible data, an exception is raised and the user is informed.

```
private var rx_buffer:ByteArray = new ByteArray();
private var bsize : int = -1;

private function onData(event:ProgressEvent):void
{
    socket.readBytes(rx_buffer, rx_buffer.length,
                     event.bytesLoaded);
    for(;;) {
        if (bsize == -1) {
            if (rx_buffer.length < 4)
                return;

            var ba : ByteArray = new ByteArray();
            rx_buffer.readBytes(ba, 0, 4);
            rx_buffer = shrinkBA(rx_buffer);
            bsize = ba.readInt();
        }

        if (rx_buffer.length < bsize)
            return;

        var pba : ByteArray = new ByteArray();
        rx_buffer.readBytes(pba, 0, bsize);
        rx_buffer = shrinkBA(rx_buffer);
        bsize = -1;

        Uplink.dispatch_packet(this, pba.readObject());
    }
}
```

The server counterpart works practically in the same way. The Storable::AMF3 module implements a simple interface. A packet after being received is decoded using the `Storable::AMF3::thaw($in)` method and for the generation of packets originating from the server the `Storable::AMF3::freeze($out)` method is used.

5.13   Interfaces

The following chapter describes various channels between the server and the client, and the data interchange format used within the session connection.

5.13.1 Session Connection Setup

As can be seen in diagram 5.16, the opening of a session connection is quite complicated process. It requires a web server and a special Flash policy server which publicly provides the current security configuration of the server. The security configuration specifies to which server ports the client can connect.

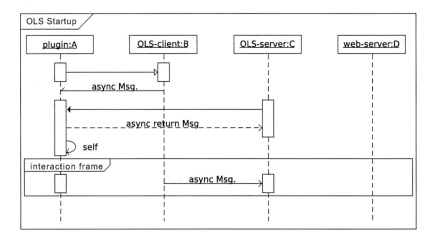

Figure 5.16: Session connection setup.

The following list describes in more detail each step which has to be accomplished before a single session socket connection can be opened. Note that for a high availability setup with more cooperating servers available, there are also multiple session connections kept open simultaneously with multiple individual server nodes forming a cloud. The servers forming the cloud will be also referred to as (server) nodes.

1. The Flash Player contacts the web server and requests the crossdomain.xml file which specifies the domains which are allowed to access the local resources.

2. The client tries to open a persistent session socket. Before doing that, a parallel TCP/IP socket to the policy server is opened by the Flash Player and the local policy information is requested and transferred in XML format. This XML file specifies which domains are allowed to open socket connections to which local ports.

83

3. Assuming that the server was properly configured and the source address complies with the given restrictions, an ordinary TCP/IP connection can be opened.

After a session connection was opened, the client introduces itself with its protocol version. The server processed this information, evaluates mutual compatibility with own protocol version and either authorizes the connection and responds to the introduction or closes the connection.

Without at least one working session connection, the client can not interact with the cloud at all. Because the initiation of the session connections takes some time and the client application is already running, the user is briefly informed about the connection progress with the cloud. There are several different states during the establishment of the cloud connection. For simplicity, the actual cloud connection state is expressed and displayed by a traffic light symbol in the background of the application.

Figure 5.17: Interpretation of the cloud connection state.

The traffic light has three different states symbolizing the overall status of the cloud connection: red, yellow, and green. Figure 5.17 shows the different states of a session connection. The application starts with no session connection open, the traffic light shows red. If there is at least one connection in the connecting or connected state, the traffic light shows yellow. If there is at least one authorized connection, the traffic light shows green and the user can authenticate. If there is at least one authenticated cloud connection, the application can start interacting with the cloud and the login window disappears.

The client application picks one authorized cloud connection and marks it as the master connection. The communication with the cloud is then performed exclusively through the master connection. First, the user authenticates itself through the master connection. A query dialog requiring a username with password is shown, the user tries to log in, and the credentials are sent to the master node. In case of a successful authentication, the master node informs the user and also other cloud nodes that the authentication succeeded. If there are authorized connections between the client and these nodes, they are automatically switched to the authenticated state. This notification is sent asynchronously to the client.

Any session connection can get disconnected at any time. If the master connection fails, the client application switches to a different authenticated session connection automatically and marks it as the new master connection. Ideally, the user does not notice anything. If there is no other authenticated connection, the process is restarted and the authentication dialog pops up again. In order to prevent the denial of service by repeated connection attempts, the client application waits after each failed connection attempt a couple of seconds. Notice containing this information is also displayed in the screen background for effortless diagnostic.

5.13.2 Network Events

Network event is a special announcement which can be transmitted completely asynchronously between the client and the server. Serialization modules on both sides create a common interface between two completely different programming environments. In both environments, the network event is treated as a hierarchical data with a predefined structure. The events can be sent in an arbitrary direction. For each direction, there is a specific data format.

Every network event sent from the client contains a command name, a sequence number, and optionally an object with command arguments. Command arguments are usually specified in an associative array.

Listing 5.11: Deserialized client-to-server event.

```
$client_event = {
    c => 'command name',
    p => $parameter_object,
    s => 1,
};
```

The server receives, deserializes, and processes the event. Upon processing of the event, depending on the command, the server may send a response back to the client. In such case, a new object is created and the original sequence number is included in the response object. The sequence is used optionally for the request-response mechanism which is needed by some functions. Other functions work completely asynchronously and ignore the sequence numbers completely.

Listing 5.12: Deserialized server-to-client response.

```
$server_response = {
    s => 1,
    r => $response_object,
};
```

In the opposite server-to-client direction, an event can be emitted also at any time. These events are used for the distribution of exceptions, during the authentication process, but mainly for the content synchronization. The content synchronization mechanism is described separately in chapter 5.14.2.

5.13.3 Network Exceptions

Network exceptions are special events which are sent from the server as a reaction to anomalous situations. A network exception can be raised as a result of a server malfunction or by an error during the processing of a request sent by the client. The exception contains a problem description and associated call stack trace. This information is displayed by the client. It is an indispensable tool for debugging purposes.

Listing 5.13: Network exception example.

```
sub _move_file($$) {
    my ( $session, $fname ) = @_;

    # Transfer the file to the media directory
    my ( $nfs, $tempname ) = File::Temp::tempfile(
        DIR    => $OLS::Config::media_dir,
        SUFFIX => OLS::generic::get_suffix($fname)
    )
    or $session->throw('Cannot create a tempfile')
    and return;

    # device independent src/dst move
    my $ret = move $fname, $tempname
    or $session->throw("move failed: $!")
    and return;

    return $tempname;
}
```

5.14 Data Organization

In this chapter the data layer and its structures will be outlined. The client mechanism used for content caching and synchronization will also be described.

An entity-relationship model was developed and implemented within a conventional SQL database in the first prototype versions. Although the SQL database was later practically substituted by the in-memory database, it is still being used as persistent data storage. This progressive transition seems to be convenient for the development of new features. They can be implemented and debugged with the SQL database which seems to be more comfortable. In a later phase of their development they can be slightly modified for use with the in-memory database. Because the SQL database initially provides all data, the SQL scheme in listing 5.14 describes also the currently used data structures and their relations.

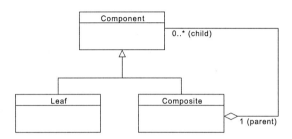

Figure 5.18: Composite pattern.

The main entity class is called the `media`. It is a generic class of all other derived classes which are understood as `media` as well. The `media` class reflects the composite pattern which can also be easily implemented in ActionScript [64] (figure 5.18). The common information stored for each medium entity are: integer identification, medium type, user identification of the creator, the time of creation, and required roles for reading and writing. There are several important derived classes: user, role, folder, question-pool, questions, combined media, file, message, chat channel, and forum. The `media` class and its relation to the surrounding classes are outlined in figure 5.19.

The system distinguishes several media groups. Some media are always organized and belong to a folder (f), certain media are always labelled and always contain a name and a description (l), and only some media are interactive and can be commented by the users (i). The type flags in parentheses are used to indicate the type of each respective medium in the following list.

- **User** (-) describes all accounts which are eventually able to access the system. For each entity, its login name, contact information, possessed roles, and the authentication method are stored.

- **Role** (l) is a simple name holder class for separate roles. A role is attached to media and users and is used during the access permission checks whenever a user tries to access a selected medium either for reading or writing.

- **Folder** (f,l) describes the name of every folder in the system. All folders are hierarchically connected and represent a spatial structure for other media.

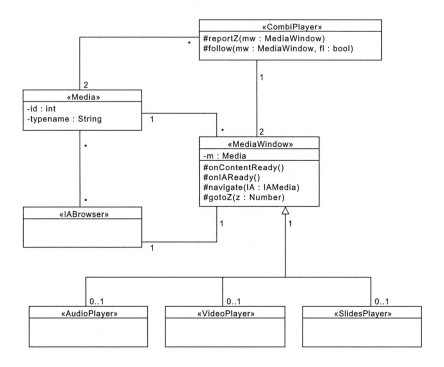

Figure 5.19: Class diagram for the basic structures and UI elements.

Each folder also has just one parent folder. The only exception is the topmost (root) folder.

- **Question pool** (f,l) is a special folder type which is either empty or contains only questions. These questions can be used by the test generator. Usually, there is one question pool within every lesson.

- **Question** (i) is a generic type of all questions within a question pool. The stored information contains the correct solution and also all answers of users to this question. The logic layer is able to compute and graphically display the correct solution. A question is always associated with just one question pool.

- **Combined media** (f,l) represents a special class used typically for synchronization of slides with an audio or a video file. It is a short record with coordinate pairs connecting time and space positions in both media files.

- **File** (f,i,l) is a generic class for downloadable content which is accessed through a common HTTP interface. As of this version, following derived classes are implemented:

- **Audio file** is an MP3 file
- **Slides file** is a specially converted PDF file
- **Video file** is a video file in a format which is supported by the Flash Player

- **Message** (-) is a short text which can be posted by users as a comment on any medium marked with the 'interactive' flag. Although the users can write a response to a message, it is not considered as an interactive medium. An answer to a message starts a conversation. Conversations are organized in threads. Interaction threads are directly associated with the interactive medium. The first message of the thread also contains the direct coordinates within the interactive medium.

- **Chat channel** (f,l) is an IRC [56] style communication facility consisting of one virtual room. This room can be simultaneously visited by different users. Users present in the room are displayed in a list which is distributed to each participant. Each chat participant can post a message at any time. The message is sent to the server via the session connection and distributed to the other participants. A short chat history is being kept by the server and distributed to the newly incoming participants. It helps to restore the context of the recent conversation. A chat channel is a form of instant messaging which can be used for troubleshooting, help, and mutual communication.

- **Forum** (f,i,l) is a classic component for mutual exchange of messages. It is either used as a browser of all comments that were made within some other interactive medium or it can be used as a direct medium in a folder for specific communication needs regarding a special topic.

Most of the media types and their user interface implementations are shown and described separately in appendix A in more detail.

For illustration, the following SQL statements are used to create the initial database structure. The structure shows also some other entity types which were not mentioned in the list of media. These classes are mostly used for auxiliary tasks, for collecting statistical data, and do not have a visible impact on the user interface.

Listing 5.14: SQL database scheme listing.

```
CREATE TABLE combi (
    id integer NOT NULL,
```

```
    md integer NOT NULL,
    mc integer NOT NULL
);

CREATE TABLE combi_content (
    id integer,
    zd integer,
    zc real
);

CREATE TABLE files (
    id integer NOT NULL,
    file text
);

CREATE TABLE folders (
    fid integer NOT NULL,
    mid integer NOT NULL,
    nr integer NOT NULL,
    v boolean DEFAULT false NOT NULL
);

CREATE TABLE im_chatlog (
    "time" timestamp without time zone,
    cid integer,
    uid integer,
    msg text
);

CREATE TABLE users (
    uid integer NOT NULL,
    uname character varying(16) NOT NULL,
    name character varying(32),
    surname character varying(32),
    mail character varying(32),
    active boolean,
    auth character varying(8)
);

CREATE TABLE interactions (
    id integer NOT NULL,
    mid integer NOT NULL,
    x real,
    y real,
    z real,
    tid integer
);

CREATE TABLE labels (
    id integer NOT NULL,
    name text,
```

```
        info text
);

CREATE TABLE lauth_passwd (
    uid integer NOT NULL,
    pw character varying(32)
);

CREATE TABLE media (
    id integer NOT NULL,
    type integer NOT NULL,
    uid integer,
    ctime timestamp without time zone
);

CREATE TABLE media_roles (
    mid integer,
    rid integer
);

CREATE TABLE media_wroles (
    mid integer,
    rid integer
);

CREATE TABLE messages (
    id integer NOT NULL,
    text text NOT NULL,
    name text NOT NULL
);

CREATE TABLE op_download (
    uid integer,
    mid integer,
    "time" timestamp without time zone
);

CREATE TABLE op_mc_option (
    uid integer,
    id integer,
    "time" timestamp without time zone,
    correct boolean
);

CREATE TABLE op_media (
    uid integer,
    mid integer,
    "time" timestamp without time zone
);

CREATE TABLE op_question (
```

```sql
    uid integer,
    id integer,
    "time" timestamp without time zone,
    score integer
);

CREATE TABLE op_session (
    id integer NOT NULL,
    starttime timestamp without time zone,
    endtime timestamp without time zone,
    nrtx integer,
    nrrx integer,
    uid integer,
    ip character varying(39),
    rxbytes integer,
    txbytes integer
);

CREATE TABLE op_slides (
    id integer,
    page integer,
    duration integer,
    uid integer,
    "time" timestamp without time zone
);

CREATE TABLE op_video (
    id integer,
    uid integer,
    "time" timestamp without time zone,
    start integer,
    stop integer
);

CREATE TABLE q_mc_options (
    id integer NOT NULL,
    qid integer,
    text text,
    hint text,
    correct boolean
);

CREATE TABLE q_mc (
    id integer NOT NULL,
    text text,
    points smallint
);

CREATE TABLE q_mc_config (
    tid integer,
    qid integer,
```

```
        oid integer,
        checked boolean,
        nr integer,
        correct boolean
);

CREATE TABLE qcoverage (
        qid integer,
        uid integer,
        count integer,
        CONSTRAINT qcoverage_count_check CHECK ((count > 0))
);

CREATE TABLE qpool (
        id integer NOT NULL,
        qpid integer
);

CREATE TABLE test_config (
        tid integer,
        qid integer,
        nr integer
);

CREATE TABLE tests (
        id integer NOT NULL,
        uid integer,
        starttime timestamp without time zone,
        endtime timestamp without time zone,
        points integer,
        score integer,
        qfid integer,
        count integer,
        deleted boolean DEFAULT false
);

CREATE TABLE types (
        id integer NOT NULL,
        name character varying(16) NOT NULL
);

CREATE TABLE users_rolemap (
        uid integer,
        rid integer
);
```

5.14.1 Content Caching

This chapter describes some implementation details of the client part which handles incoming events regarding changing media in the cloud. A medium after being received stays persistent in the operating memory of the client in order to prevent repeated transmission of the same data. This greatly improves the responsiveness of the application and it also reduces the network and system loads. Listing 5.15 shows the implementation of the media class which is used for caching purposes by the client. The media cache structure works as a special in-memory database within the client application while at least one authenticated connection with the cloud exists. If the last authenticated connection is lost, the complete media cache is discarded.

Listing 5.15: ActionScript media class used for caching purposes.

```
public class Media
{
        public var id : uint;              // media id
        public var ctime : uint;           // creation time (epoch)
        public var author : String;        // author's name
        public var name : String;          // content's name
        public var info : String;          // optional description
        public var typename : String;      // media type
        public var pid : uint;        // parent id
        public var tid : uint;        // target media
        public var c : Array;         // opt. array of children
        public var x : Number;        // opt. placement coordinates
        public var y : Number;
        public var z : Number;
        public var nr : int;               // number in folder structure
        public var v : Boolean;            // visibility flag
        public var ia : Boolean;           // tid defined => IA
}
```

Because the content is organized fully hierarchically, the first request sent from the client is the 'get content' query of media with ID 0. This is a reserved value for the root folder which contains everything other. The global folder structure is processed and a new personalised folder structure is generated and sent back to the client. The personalized structure is created individually for each user according to the user and media access permissions. The client application creates a new media structure and fills it with this data. Since that point in time is the media cached and instantly available for any further access. The session connection is used exclusively for this kind of communication. Further modifications of the media cache are performed only after receiving a synchronization event from the cloud.

94

5.14.2 Synchronization Events

Whenever a special media event occurs, like a content or visibility modification, a deletion, or access permissions change, the server identifies all users for which this change is relevant and informs them accordingly with an appropriate event. The cloud works with the following events:

- **ADD** is emitted whenever a new readable content is published.

- **UPDATE** is emitted whenever a readable content is modified.

- **DELETE** is emitted whenever a readable content is deleted or made not readable anymore for the respective client.

Listing 5.16: Deserialized server broadcast event.

```
$server_broadcast = {
    b => 'event name',
    p => $parameter_object,
};
```

For instance, for an administrator the visibility change (turn to invisible) of a medium is a relatively unimportant information. An UPDATE event would be sent to such user. But for an ordinary participant such a change causes the emission of the DELETE event because it virtually seems that the content was deleted. In both cases the client's media is cache notified, by the administrator the media structure is modified and the v bit unset, while in the basic learning interface, the medium record is released from the media cache completely. All changes are instantly reflected also in the user interface.

5.14.3 Access Permission Checking

Each medium contains two categories of access information for reading and writing. Each one is an unordered list of roles which have to be possessed by the user. If the user does not feature at least all roles required by a medium, the access is denied and an exception is generated. The implementation of such mechanism is quite simple and allows configurations which are usually required for complex learning setups offering more courses for various groups of students. There are also two special administrative roles. The 'admin' and 'superadmin' roles are always required for administrative tasks with the content, the latter is required for operations with roles and user accounts.

5.14.4 User Management

User account operations can be performed by the users with the 'superadmin' role and according to the configuration, new user accounts can also be added automatically after a successful authentication by a third-party system. The authentication can be configured very modularly and it can combine more authentication methods at once. For the administrative users, the authentication is typically performed against the local database, other modules are then available for LDAP or Ilias databases. In such case the system allows comfortable access of university users with their own campus password or access of distant users from other institutions in general.

5.15 Software Footprint

The following chapter provides a short overview of the client and the server regarding the internal structure. Although it is difficult to provide some kind of an extensive comparison of the client and the server with other products, figure 5.20 summarizes some elementary information[5] including the sizes of the executable data and lines of code written for each component.

Module	Language	LOC	Binary Size
Basic Frontend	AS3	13657	1.7 MB
Administrative Console	AS3	3569	3.5 MB
Server Application	Perl	9964	238 KB

Figure 5.20: Source code metrics of the server and the client.

5.15.1 Server

The server implementation was written completely in Perl. It uses utilizes many modules from several different authors. It is a multithreaded application using the standard Perl threads implementation. Each thread deals with a specific task.

- The **main thread** is initially started with the application and prepares and starts all other threads. It also detects program failures which could occur in some thread and cause it to terminate. In such case the application is terminated completely and the details are protocoled. This allows automated restarts of the whole server.

---

[5] As of 19th June 2013.

- The **uplink thread** handles all session connections with the clients. It accepts new connections and hands them over to the client thread.

- The **client thread** is a special thread which processes all data received from the session connections. It controls the input/output queue for each client separately, performs the packet de-/serialization, and executes corresponding routines with each incoming event.

- The **mailer thread** is responsible for SMTP [40] communication with the users. Participants of a conversation with a new posting are notified automatically by the system. The outgoing mail queue is handled completely by this thread.

- The **policy thread** represents an implementation of a tiny file server used for the distribution of the policy file which is required by the Flash Player before a session connection can be opened. The policy file contains a short information to which ports and from which domains incoming connections are allowed.

- The **wipc** thread handles the interprocess communication with the associated web interface. It receives and forwards authentication data and download requests to the client thread. The interprocess communication is done via a local stream socket.

5.15.2   Client

The client was completely developed using various versions of the Flex SDK. It consists of two separate modules. The basic learning module which is loaded initially and implements the functionality of the basic learning interface. The administrative interface is compiled separately, downloaded and executed on demand by the content and system administrators. Figure 5.21 summarizes the major use-cases of the whole system.

5.16   Scalability and Extensibility

In electronics (including hardware, communication, and software), scalability is the ability of a system, network, or process, to handle a growing amount of work in a capable manner or its ability to be enlarged to accommodate that growth [8].

The client incorporates support for multiple simultaneous server connections and it is able to switch dynamically among them, whenever the active master connection fails. The servers share the same data and form together a cloud. In case of a connection handover, when a client switches to another server, the user should not be ideally aware of any difference. Design of an experimental server prototype for such a configuration is described in chapter 7.2.3 on page 102.

5.17 Maintenance

Maintenance of the server software is a part of the software life cycle. It includes consecutive bug fixing and troubleshooting resulting in code modifications of both components, the client and the server. The major advantage of the actualization of the client application is its HTTP distribution channel. After a release, old binary files are simply replaced on the web server and downloaded by the web browsers automatically on the next occasion.

So long a certain version persists on the server, it is also cached by the web browser and ideally downloaded only once. The caching guarantees that the consecutive startups are correspondingly faster. Each client introduces itself during the session connection authorization with its session protocol version. In case that an obsolete version number is detected, the server forces the browser to download the latest version of the client application.

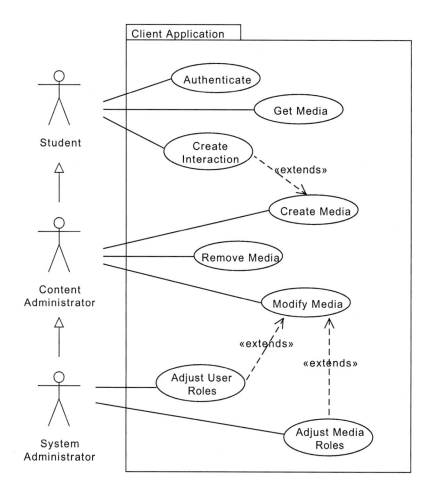

Figure 5.21: Use-case diagram for the client application.

Chapter 6

Systems Compared

This chapter describes a detailed comparison of the Ilias LMS with the newly developed system with the major focus on issues which were identified in the the Ilias system evaluations. Although not all functions which are present in the current Ilias version were implemented in the new system, the latest versions of the software include all features that are required in the online courses. On the one hand, the new system is theoretically capable of substituting Ilias, but on the other hand, more interestingly, this stage opens a way for direct performance testing and various comparisons of both systems.

6.1 Evaluation

The user interface of the new client application was evaluated using several cognitive walkthroughs with different groups of persons ranging from computer literates with no previous experience with an e-learning system to professional e-learning system administrators. Stones et al. [73] describe a cognitive walkthrough as a process that evaluates *"the steps required to perform a task and attempts to uncover mismatches between how the users think about a task and how the UI designer thinks about the task"*.

Specific issues that appeared during the Ilias evaluation were already described in a separate chapter (chapter 4.5) and they were divided into generic problem classes. The following survey describes how each separate issue is handled by the new system.

6.1.1 Heterogeneity

During the cognitive walkthrough experiment, the participants had to open a lecture and post own comments to slides, audio, and video files. The locations where the comments should have been made were also specified.

In the new system, the access to various media types is unified through the basic learning interface. When posting a comment, the application switches to the 'question mode'. After a mouse click, the exact click coordinates are detected automatically for any interactive medium type by the universal interactivity layer. It is a transparent layer shown over slides and videos. The layer is synchronized with the current playing position of the underlying medium. As coordinates, the page number of the current slide or the current playing time position in a video or an audio file are used. In the 'question mode', the layer reacts on mouse clicks. The click position is recalculated to media coordinates. Question composer is opened, the message is formulated, associated with the coordinates, and finally sent to the server.

Other participants are notified of the new posting either through a special window showing the latest changes and interactions within the system or if they have the same document opened, the new posting appears immediately in the respective media player. The next feature of the interactivity layer is to display interactions of other participants as speech bubbles. Upon clicking on a speech bubble, a window with the posting and the associated conversation thread are shown. The user can read or join the conversation directly.

Course participants have also the possibility to create a dynamic conversation structure associated to any interactive medium. The administrators can control the growth of the conversation thread either by active participation in the discussions or by removing the redundant and unwanted conversation threads. For security reasons the postings are stored in a separate database structure. The structure is also derived from the composite pattern of the static content. Both contents are merged together by the client which virtually combines these two sources as one large structure. The joint structure is shown in figure 6.1. The difference to the Ilias interpretation as can be seen in figure 4.5 on page 44 is obvious.

According to the cognitive walkthroughs, the increased generalization of the data structures and the ability to start a dialogue practically anywhere within any interactive medium seems to be the one of the greatest usability benefits reducing the communication overhead significantly. There is no need to describe the coordinates with own words and reciprocally to interpret such descriptions. But at the same time, there is only one way how new interactions can be posted.

A minor problem during the testing was unintentionally sent postings which can be removed only by the administrators.

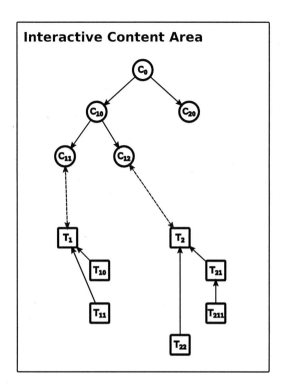

Figure 6.1: Arrangement model of the new system.

6.1.2 Test Generator

The test generator produces test exams which try to imitate their original paper form. This together with the fact that each user can generate and postpone multiple tests simultaneously, was positively accepted by the participants. The possibility of commenting on single questions and even their parts (individual options of multiple-choice questions) substantially speeded up the communication in the threads associated with a question or its part.

Problematic questions can be detected by the system automatically. The system computes the global statistics for each question. The number of times it was answered wrong and the number of times it appeared in a test represent the fail rate which can be used for the evaluation of question pools. The same can be conducted for parts of some questions. Questions with high fail rates can require a special attention since they are difficult to answer which could be also caused by an ambiguous or wrong formulation, etc.

Intentionally wrong option of a multiple-choice question was included in a question pool during a special experiment. Due to the outstanding fail rates, the problematic question and its option could be clearly identified through the noticeable high fail rate at the end of the experiment. There were only 20 participants answering the question.

6.1.3 Response Latency

The original purpose of the experiment mentioned in the previous chapter was to check the response latency problem. The measurement summarizes the total number of requests, bytes received, and bytes sent by the client application during the generation, completion, submission, and review of a test. During the experiment, the participants were not allowed to scroll through the questions in Ilias which would generate an additional traffic. Each question had to be answered immediately. The test contained ten multiple-choice questions which were used in both systems. Table 6.2 shows a direct comparison during this experiment. Note that the Ilias system uses the deflate compression mechanism. The prototype does not compress the transmitted and received data at all.

The prototype generates only three requests during the process. Each request has to be processed by the server synchronously and each is associated with a waiting time:

1. request the generation of a test

2. submit the answers

3. request the results

The major delay is caused during the test generation. Unfortunately, this delay could not be measured precisely but the reaction was perceived as instant. After the test is completely answered, the solution is submitted. The client application then requests the results automatically and displays the correct solution eventually with marked mistakes.

The Ilias system sends a request after each click, waits for a response, displays the next question, etc. Totally, there were 12 clicks needed for the completion of the test. The number of requests sent shows the sum of all GET and POST requests that were sent by a single client.

The exam experiment shows a notable difference between both platforms. While the thin client requests data after each mouse click, the RIA utilizes a content caching mechanism and communicates with the server only in necessary cases. Accordingly high is then the number of requests and the amount

	Prototype	Ilias
requests sent	3	34
bytes sent	104	28226
bytes received	4257	113314[a]

[a]Compressed size, uncompressed size is appx. 700 KB.

Figure 6.2: Exam experiment summary.

of transferred data which can also include graphic elements of individual web pages. Although the thin client may utilize the caching mechanism of the web browser, the RIA offers much wider space for various additional optimizations using custom logic.

6.1.4   Availability

The left bottom corner of the prototype shows the traffic light symbol displaying the overall status of all session connections with the cloud, and also informs about the connection progress in textual form. Due to the significantly lower memory consumption (approximately 256 bytes per connection + operating system resources for every opened TCP/IP connection), the operating memory can not get easily exhausted and the prototype does not collapse because of a memory shortage, since there are other system restrictions like the maximum number of file descriptors. However, higher complexity opens a space to higher amount of software bugs which can lead to a malfunction of the prototype. It seems that only long-term testing can help uncovering most of them.

6.1.5   Other Feedback

The prototype system allows downloading of any data which is stored as a file on the server. After a successful permission check, the download is started via an ordinary HTTP connection. The testing has shown that there is a demand for downloading of other media types from the system. Combined media, media with embedded comments, and generated tests could be exported to reasonable formats and offered for download. These export features could be developed as additional server modules and only minimal modification of the source code of the server would probably be required.

The evaluations of the user interface pointed out several usability problems and also suggested several improvements, like the missing search function within the complete system and especially the missing local search within the slides player. Missing possibility of making personal notes in the system, and many others. Again, it seems that these features could be easily developed in the next application versions.

6.2 Overload Simulation

In the following experiment, a special test scenario was prepared. The scenario should replicate the situation which caused the high load before the exams in a shorter simulation time.

By analyzing the Ilias system during the time, the typical user behaviour was discovered. Accordingly, a test scenario representing the user behaviour during the day was prepared. This scenario was used during the experiment which should replicate the high system load as can be seen in figure 4.6 on page 47 and in figure 4.7 on page 48. The measurements were conducted with multiple different hardware configurations.

During the preparation of the experiment, the complete course was exported from Ilias in the SCORM format and imported into the prototype. An external application running on a remote computer was used to simulate 128 active virtual users. Each virtual user performs 128 elementary operations. Each operation represents a basic interaction with the system like browsing the folder structure or accessing the course data. The operations are executed sequentially, each virtual user waits one second after each operation. The operation delay of an ordinary human user varies between 1 second and 10 minutes, estimated mean time is 6 seconds.

Figure 6.3 shows the average one-minute loads which were generated by various systems and also the durations which were required to accomplish the simulation. The most surprising is the result of the Raspberry Pi which not only surpassed the ordinary server with Ilias during this experiment, but it also did not get overloaded.

Table 6.4 shows a substantial difference between the original Ilias system and the new prototype. The prototype system performed better than Ilias because of lower code complexity and especially because of the sophisticated content caching performed actively by the clients. Within the Ilias system, there was a significant CPU time consumed by the SQL database which was literally braking out other processes.

During the continuation of the experiment only with the prototype on the reference hardware, the configuration was changed. Newly, 1024 simultaneous clients were simulated. The test application was executed on eight workstations, each simulating 128 clients. This separation was made in order to prevent an excessive load of the workstation computers. Even under such conditions, the CPU of the reference system remained underloaded.

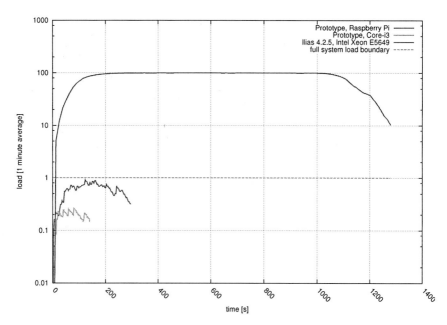

Figure 6.3: Loads of multiple systems in comparison.

As can be seen in figure 6.5, the simulation with over 1000 connections takes a slightly more time and also the host system requires some special adjustments. These adjustments are necessary for increasing of the maximum allowed number of connections. This property is determined by the maximum allowed number of file descriptors and other operating system specific internal variables.

Software	CPU	RAM (GB)	Time Elapsed (s)	Load Peak	Mean Power Consumption (W)
Ilias 4.2.5	Xeon E5649	8	1280	100	243
Prototype	Core i3-2367M	8	140	0.26	17
Prototype	ARM1176JZF-S	0.25	300	0.92	3

Figure 6.4: Load measurement summary.

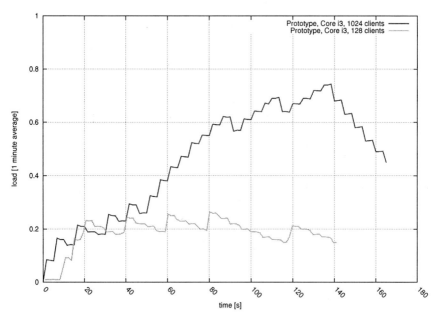

Figure 6.5: Simulations with the prototype with 1024 and 128 connections.

108

Chapter 7

Conclusion

This chapter summarizes the past development, points out some interesting interfaces and experimental features, and briefly reviews the advantages and disadvantages of the new concept.

7.1 Improving Existing LAMP Systems

Improving existing systems may aim either to increase the system performance, or to render the system more flexible in terms of programming techniques and extensions possibilities. The incorporation of the prototype framework into an existing system with a plain LAMP architecture as shown in figure 4.3 can be easily achieved by implementation of a local communication endpoint for data interchange with the session server. The session server can be easily customized and reprogrammed to support selected tasks with optional utilization of the in-memory database. This concept is generally suitable for systems with a high read/write ratio and it can also be utilized for the development of a new software from scratch.

7.2 Further Development and Possibilities

This section briefly discusses some interesting interfaces and performed experiments which promise interesting possibilities for the further development.

7.2.1 Extended Content Evaluation

The prototype records the access count, the view duration, and the count of comments for every interactive medium. Although this list may seem exhaustive, there are several possibilities in which this data gathering can be deepened. For a specific content evaluation of slides and videos an eye tracking interface can be easily adopted. Nielsen et al. [52] introduce so called eye-mind hypothesis stating that *"people are usually thinking about what they are looking at. They do not always totally or engage with it, but if they are looking, they are usually paying attention, especially when concentrating on a particular task."* This hypothesis seems legitimate also for online slides and particular learning videos. One possible interpretation of the eye tracking analysis is the so-called heat map. It is a function describing the total duration which the eyes have spent on each possible spot within a medium. The result of such measurement represents a very interesting option for further improvement of the learning material. Currently, there are several open projects which are able to perform the eye tracking analysis using even a common web camera. This is a low-cost option for interesting home experiments.

7.2.2 Advanced Automated Testing

The automated testing module offers interesting interfaces which can be used for question evaluation on per participant basis. There is a sufficient amount of data stored for the individual estimation of ability and attitude. On this basis, individual tests with suitable questions can be generated which could lead to a better user experience and to a better learning effect. In present version, there is only a simple test pool coverage monitoring implemented, so that every test participant get yet unanswered questions in every new generated test and already answered questions are not repeated in further tests. Albeit the extension of the assessment module may seem as an interesting option, required computation difficulty, stability, and eventual new security issues can be seen as negative impacts on the server software and have to be well taken into account.

7.2.3 High Availability Extensions

This chapter focuses on some interesting experimental features resulting from possible multi-nodal cloud configurations.

The client session connection stack was slightly generalized and extended in order to maintain not only one but multiple session connections with multiple servers nodes at once. Because each client communicates only with the master node, the server-to-server connections are used to forward and spread the incoming events in the cloud.

There are two types of server nodes which can participate in a cloud: active and passive. Active nodes are allowed to create a new content upon a request from a client, whilst passive nodes are not permitted to create anything in the cloud. Passive nodes are used only for read-only operations and their purpose is data replication. Each active node has a cloud identification number. The identification number is stored in the configuration file of every server node. The state of a cloud with multiple nodes which are not mutually connected is called the 'split mode' (figure 7.1[1]).

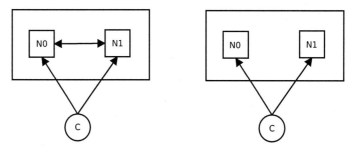

Figure 7.1: Normal and split cloud modes.

The content of an e-learning system consists typically of high amount of media records and is stored on every cloud server in multiple databases. Thanks to the high level of used generalization in the prototype framework, media records store and describe everything in the system, including user accounts, specific server settings, directory structures, access permissions, etc. Each medium record is also uniquely identified by an integer number. Because the media records can be created simultaneously on different nodes which are eventually in the split mode, each active node configuration contains a predefined node number n $(n \in Z)$ which is used during the creation of the new media records. Let t be the total number of nodes in a cloud configuration. Let M_n be a set of media identifiers created and used by node n. A new unique m_{id} identification of the next created medium record will be determined as

$$m_{id} = \begin{cases} n & \text{for} \quad M_n = \emptyset \\ max(M_n) + t & \text{for} \quad M_n \neq \emptyset \end{cases}$$

This simple mechanism keeps the medium record identifiers separated in residue classes and guarantees a collision-free creation and manipulation with the media records on all server nodes. In case that not all server nodes are available, the client should still be able to use the system for read operations. Since there is yet no collision solving algorithm, modification and deletion of media records can only be performed by nodes where they were originally created, which means that under certain circumstances the cloud can not perform such an operation in the split mode.

---

[1]C – client, N0, N1 – server nodes.

Content Mirroring

After a successful server-to-server connection, the synchronization phase begins. Hereby the created, modified, and deleted m_{id} numbers are exchanged and the unsynchronized media records are detected and transmitted. This activity runs completely in the background which means that the node can serve clients and operate in in a usual manner.

In order to avoid collisions and conflicts resolutions, the content can be directly modified and deleted only by the nodes on which it was originally created. If there is a request for modification or removal on a different cloud node, a network event is created and sent to the original author node which performs the required operation.

In order to prevent cloud misconfiguration like unwanted connections of nodes from different clouds, each server-to-server connection has to be verified and authorized with a simple passphrase check.

Content mirroring also allows data transitions to passive servers that can be used as accelerating proxies or as fully dedicated backup servers which eventually do not serve any client connection.

Seamless Upgrades

Configurations with multiple server nodes offer interesting possibilities in the server software update process. If planned, prepared, and performed properly, sequential update of multiple cloud nodes does not interrupt the individual cloud connections of the clients. Each node can be turned off and its software updated with a newer version. After the update, the node is started again and rejoins the cloud. The most important requirement is the backward compatibility of the server-to-server connection. This mechanism eventually also allows to revert the update and roll back to the previous software version.

If the whole cloud is updated sequentially and the system administrator proceeds with the update cautiously, the clients eventually do not loose the cloud connection since they reconnect to the updated cloud nodes automatically.

The next utilization of this feature is the partial upgrade. Partial upgrade means that only some but not all server nodes are updated. Updated nodes might contain experimental modifications that can be tested with the real users. Access to the updated nodes can be for practical reasons restricted on the IP-level with a packet filter. Multi-nodal setups can of course also exist concurrently on a single computer lacking the high availability option in case of a hardware failure but with the option of seamless upgrades preserved.

7.2.4 Solar Cloud

The Raspberry Pi, introduced in chapter 5.8.2, with a consumption below 3 Watt can be easily powered by the Sun from a small photovoltaic cell. With a backup battery and a proper charging circuit, the device is able to run permanently consuming only solar power. Balfour et al. [4] offer useful tips for proper design of the whole circuit. A more interesting configuration consists of multiple nodes with a suitable geographical placement. According to the position of the Sun only some nodes are powered at a particular daytime. As described in chapter 7.2.3, newly started nodes join the cloud and obtain a copy of the database and vice versa, nodes loosing the solar power are leaving the cloud spontaneously. According to the estimation of Koomey [41], the whole internet infrastructure consumed 14 GW of power already in 2005. According to the more recent estimations, the infrastructure consumption reaches 30 GW in 2012 [10]. Although the generation of electricity from photovoltaics can be seen as controversial since the photovoltaics industry seems to be the net consumer till 2015 [17], there are also different methods for solar-thermal-electric power generation [19]. This configuration remains very promising but represents more an engineering curiosity and a technical challenge rather than a feasible, green, and truly nature-friendly solution.

7.3 Summary

A new web e-learning system was developed from scratch as a rich internet application (RIA). The initial motive for the development was to deal with issues of the existing Ilias learning management system environment which has been used for multiple years in several courses. User experience and multiple tests and evaluations helped with the identification of various issues including low performance, and several usability and interactivity related problems. The fundamental assumption that the identical hardware should be able to provide the same service without the mentioned issues, leads to the establishment of an architecture utilizing session connections and in-memory databases and to the development of a completely new system. The core architecture is primarily intended for e-learning solutions but it can be easily reused for implementation of further generic information systems or for various modifications of existing ones.

Albeit the new prototype includes only a subset of functions that are currently implemented in recent Ilias versions, it implements all functions that have been used in online courses. Therefore, the new prototype could theoretically be used as an Ilias replacement. In order to confirm this assumption, the prototype was run in parallel to Ilias offering the same content for the purpose of evaluation and testing of individual features during the past years.

The testing confirmed that the communication overhead caused by various function parts of the whole system is lower than by Ilias. Thanks to the RIA concept, the substantial part of logic could have been moved from the server to the client application. This step reduced the software complexity of the server code and also minimized the amount of data transmitted through the network. User interface evaluation has shown that several issues could have been resolved by the utilization of the RIA-specific features and by the introduction of the general interactive layer. This virtual layer avoids the communication overhead and enables a straightforward instant commenting of arbitrary media anywhere within the system. By computing the access, commentary, and fail rate statistics for each medium and place, the most problematic contents and their parts respectively, can be identified and reported automatically. This kind of feedback is valuable for the consequential improvement of the learning content.

A simulation has shown that the prototype is able to serve more than 1000 clients simultaneously without causing CPU overload of the host system. Contrary to Ilias using a plain LAMP thin client architecture handling 128 simultaneous connections with a significant overload on a midrange server, the prototype has achieved the same task without overload even on a server with much less powerful hardware configuration. The hardware requirements are modest and the software is capable of running on the Raspberry Pi single board computer which provides a noteworthy performance running the prototype with only a minimal power consumption.

Although the new concept provides some advantages over the plain thin client architecture, there are several drawbacks which should be remembered. The persistent presence of an additional server for the management of session connections is mandatory and increases the complexity of the server software substantially, opening a space for new security threats. On the other hand, the bidirectional asynchronous session connection offers challenging possibilities for the further development of new features using event-based programming.

The specific architecture also enabled the support for server-to-server and multiple client-to-server connections. Proper configuration with multiple server nodes organized in a cloud represents a specific form of a backup method. The cloud can increase the overall system reliability and opens new possibilities for the system administration and maintenance.

Limitations resulting from using a non-HTTP protocol persist also in cloud configurations. The testing has shown some rare cases when users fail to connect to the cloud because of specific network conditions. Such cases include firewall misconfiguration and rather restrictive network configurations, generally allowing only web traffic. The testing has also shown that a typical user working at home or at the university is able to access the system without problems. The required computer equipment includes a web browser with a recent Flash Player version.

Like many open source projects, in the first days the project is owned and maintained only by one person. A numerous user base is essential for the eventual further development and sustainability of the project. Attracting new users, developers, and building of a surrounding community might be yet much harder than the development of the initial prototype and represents a strong challenge for the future.

Notice

The project was named Ὀδύσσεια :: Interactive E-learning System and made publicly available as free open source software.

The project page can be found at

$$http://code.google.com/p/ol5/$$

Appendix A

The Client

The following chapters deal with various controls and features of the client application.

Introduction

The client application consists of two parts. It is the basic learning module and the administrative interface which is loaded on demand. For proper function, the Flash Player extension has to be installed.

Compilation

The application can be compiled using Apache Flex. Currently, version 4.9 is used for the compilation. Once properly set up, add the `bin` directory to the system `PATH` variable and compile the project with the `make` command.

Installation

There are no special steps required for the installation. Binary SWF files have to be copied properly in the web server directory structure as described in chapter B.2.2.

A.1 Basic Interface

Once opened, the browser downloads the application binary and executes it within the Flash Player extension. The download progress is displayed in the middle of the screen with a small progress bar. According to the connection speed, the download process can take several seconds. After a successful download, the application is started immediately and the login window is displayed (figure A.1).

Figure A.1: Login window.

The application obtains the cloud configuration from the server and tries to open the session connections to several cloud nodes. The cloud connection progress is displayed in the left-bottom corner with a short textual information (figure A.2). The traffic light symbol summarizes the overall cloud connection state. The green color indicates that there is at least one active cloud connection. The yellow color means that there is a connection process pending. And the red color means that either the client fails to connect and waits for a few seconds before trying to reconnect or the cloud is improperly configured and the client will not work at all.

Figure A.2: Cloud connection status.

After the cloud connection is established, the traffic light shows green and the login button gets enabled. The user may now be authenticated. After a successful authentication, the login window disappears and the basic browser window is displayed.

Every window contains the basic controls in the top-right corner for minimizing, maximizing, and closing. According to the window type, some of these controls can be eventually hidden.

Windows in minimized state are shown in the bottom part of the screen in the left to right direction. A minimized window can be restored to the normal state by double clicking on its title bar.

By right-clicking on the title bar of the browser window, a context menu is displayed (figure A.3). The menu offers the basic operations for minimizing, maximizing, and restoring size of particular windows, but there are also several further window manipulation actions, offering various arrangements of all displayed windows (tile, cascade) and manipulation with all present windows (show all windows).

Figure A.3: Context menu of a window.

A.1.1 Browser

The main browser window in figure A.4 displays the content structure organized in folders. Every folder can get closed or unfolded by single clicking on the small triangle preceding the folder symbol. An arbitrary item can be chosen from the folder structure. Selected item is then highlighted with a blue background. The lower part of the browser window shows a short description of the selected item. If the item is runnable, the start button becomes active and the content can be shown either by clicking on the start button or by double clicking directly on the item. In case that the content is downloadable, the Download button becomes active.

The browser window contains a few more miscellaneous controls, the menu bar where the administrative console can be started and the application log window can be shown. The text address bar can be used for navigating to an `ols://`

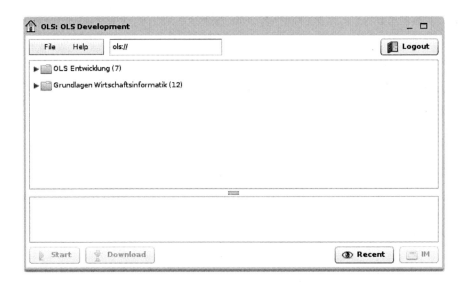

Figure A.4: Default browser window.

address, and similarly after selecting an item, its address is generated and shown in the address bar. This type of address is convenient during the communication with other participants in external channels like email or instant messaging. In the right-bottom corner, there is a 'Recent' button which displays so called recent browser. The recent browser contains a chronologically sorted list of the last interactions. A double click on any entry opens an 'Interactions Browser' window with the selected comment.

A.1.2 Interactions Browser

The 'Interactions Browser' is the basic interface for mutual communication in the entire application. It allows the exchange of textual messages among multiple users. Inspired by email communication, each message contains a subject, a brief summary of the topic, and the message body. The communication flow is displayed in the bottom half of the window (figure A.5). The upper window part displays the content of the currently selected message. Interactions Browser is used for all interactions within the individual players of multimedia files. Pure interactions are displayed as speech bubbles in media players. Figure A.9 shows a PDF document with one interaction. The interaction browser can be also used completely separately as a forum. Forums have their own entry in the folder structure.

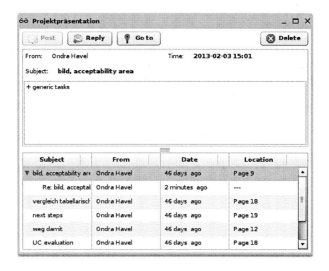

Figure A.5: Interactions browser window.

Buttons in the top part are used for posting of new messages (the 'Post' button which is only active in forums and allows starting of a new thread), 'Reply' button is used for answering to the currently selected message, 'Go to' button opens the associated media player window (if any) and jumps to the position where the comment was made. The 'Delete' button is visible only for administrators which can remove the selected message.

New interactions can be created with the Question Composer (figure A.6). It is a simple rich-text editor which can be launched either by the "Interactions Browser" or by a media player upon user request.

A.1.3   Chatroom

A chatroom offers a space primarily for communication of multiple users in real-time. Figure A.7 shows a sample chatroom window. The left part contains the conversation, the user can interact by formulating own sentence in the bottom text input. After the enter key is pressed, the message is sent to the server which then distributes it to other chat participants. User names which are present in the chatroom are displayed in the list on the right side. The chat component restores a few lines of the recent conversation to the newly incoming users.

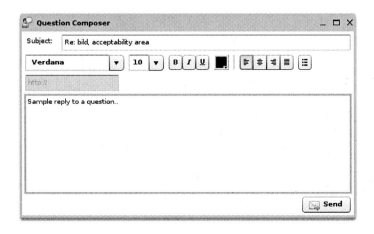

Figure A.6: Question composer window.

A.1.4 Basic Interaction Controls

Figure A.8 shows a group of buttons used in most media players for posting and controlling the visibility of the interactions. The first button opens the interactions browser with a summary of all comments made in the medium. The second – toggle button – disables or enables the overlay display of speech bubbles in the medium. Finally, the third button switches the cursor into the 'question mode' mode and the user can now click anywhere in the medium to create and post a new comment. Upon clicking in the 'question mode', the composer window with associated coordinates is shown and the comment can be written and sent.

A.1.5 Slides Player

Slides player (figure A.9) is a plain browser capable of displaying the imported PDF files. It allows basic zooming and fitting of the content. Zoomed content can be panned with the mouse.

A.1.6 Video Player

Video player (figure A.10) is capable of playback of video formats supported by the Flash Player. It also includes the same layer for the creation of new comments during the playback. Other controls are standard and can be found in most common video players as well. The gray box in the seek bar indicates

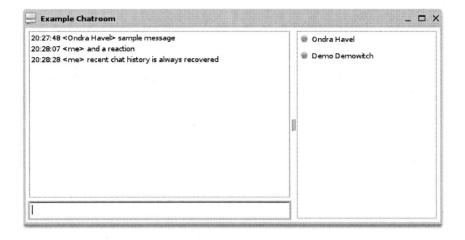

Figure A.7: Chatroom window.

Figure A.8: Basic interaction controls.

the video loading progress. Unfortunately, seeking behind the loaded progress is currently not possible.

A.1.7 Audio Player

Audio player (figure A.11) is used exclusively for playback of MP3 files. A new comment can be posted at the current playing time position which is indicated by the seek bar. The seek bar shares the same concept with the video player.

A.1.8 Combined Player

There are two types of multimedia files distinguished by the system:

- media with continuous time : audio, video

- media with discrete time : slides

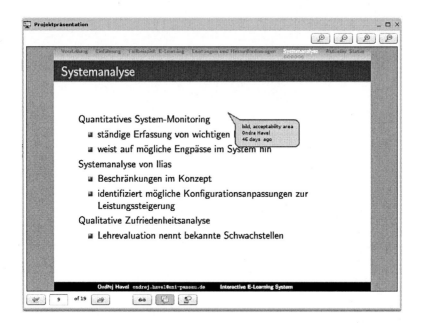

Figure A.9: Slides player.

Using a combined player, the discrete time media can be played back in synchronization with a continuous time media. The time position of the discrete media is switched automatically according to the actual time of the continuous medium. The process works also in the opposite way. Whenever the user changes position of the discrete time medium in its player, the position of the continuous time medium is adjusted accordingly. Each media player is extended with a *Sync* checkbox which determines, if the player can be controlled by the associated player during the combined playback. This extension (usually placed in the right-bottom corner) can be seen in figure A.15.

A.1.9 Test Generator

The test generator works with question pools. A question pool is a special folder containing only questions of various types. In the test explorer window (figure A.12), the user can generate a new test with a specified amount of questions, continue a postponed test, or review a completed test. The window also shows how many questions reside in the question pool and how many of them have been answered at least once (question pool coverage). During the generation of a new test, primarily new and yet unanswered questions are preferred.

126

Figure A.10: Video player.

Figure A.11: Audio player.

The generated test is displayed in a separate window (figure A.13) and segmented in multiple pages in order to resemble the paper version. Control buttons of the test window at the bottom side allow pages flipping, postponing of the test, and commenting. Commenting is only available in the review mode with an already submitted test.

A.2 Administrative Interface

The administrative interface can be loaded after clicking at a relevant menu item in the basic interface browser. The user has to have the *admin* role assigned. The administrative interface is based on the basic interface with slight enhancements. The extended menu bar contains operations for new or selected media, the 'Ad-

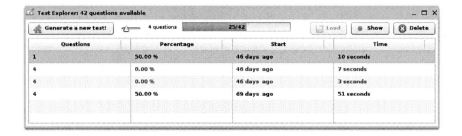

Questions	Percentage	Start	Time
1	50.00 %	46 days ago	10 seconds
4	0.00 %	46 days ago	7 seconds
4	0.00 %	46 days ago	3 seconds
4	50.00 %	69 days ago	51 seconds

Figure A.12: Test explorer.

minister' menu item then contains operations for users and roles management. In the bottom-right part of the window, next to the description area of the selected medium, the up and down, and visibility buttons are located.

The up and down buttons are used for adjusting the position of the selected medium in its folder, the visibility toggle button shows or hides the selected media to non-administrative users. Hidden media are always shown in the administrative interface. Multiple media can be selected by clicking and holding the shift key to select a range of media or by clicking and holding the ctrl key to toggle the selection of a single media. Only some operations will work with multiple media selected.

A.2.1 Access Control

The system provides a simple media role-based access control mechanism. A role is a labelled ancillary medium which can be assigned to users and content media. Roles are primarily a way of grouping multiple users and assigning permissions to that group. Any user can have multiple different roles assigned. Each media possess two sets of roles for read and write access which are required during the permission checks.

The permission checking is a simple process. The system discovers roles of the requested medium and of all its parent folders. It then checks whether the user has all these roles assigned and if so, it allows the access. Otherwise, an exception is thrown and the access is denied. The mechanism works the same for reading and writing. For writing, the read access is also checked as prerequisite.

A.2.2 Media Operations

The following chapter summarizes the basic operations for creating, import, and manipulation with media. New media can be either directly created in the system

Figure A.13: Test review.

or uploaded via the upload manager. The upload manager is capable of uploading multiple files consecutively. Supported formats are: PDF (slides), videos in formats supported by the Flash Player, and Ilias SCORM export archives. After uploading the files, the import process is started. After its completion, the import result is displayed in the log window which appears automatically.

For the creation of new media directly in the application a generic window is displayed. Using this window, mandatory information has to be inputted. Each medium has a name, an optional description, and always belongs to a folder. The rename command allows later change of the name and the description. The move command changes the parent folder of selected media.

The delete function supports the removal of multiple selected media. After confirmation, the system attempts to delete the listed media. The result is shown in the table for each selected medium.

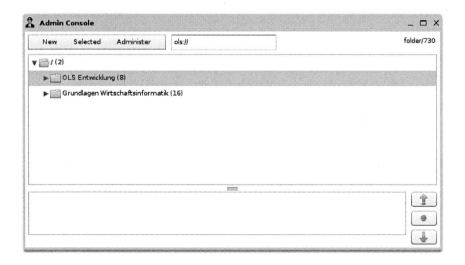

Figure A.14: Administrative window.

A.2.3 Media Evaluation

The evaluation tool is capable of generating charts for selected media. The chart displays for each playing time or position the number of times the medium was visited or commented. For question pools additionally, the fail rate of each question is computed. Results of this evaluation are very beneficial for finding of problematic content within the system.

A.2.4 Combined Editor

The combined editor (figure A.15) allows the creation and manipulation of synchronized media pairs. The editor utilizes the common media players and shows an additional window where the synchronization can be set and adjusted. The file-menu contains the basic operations for saving, initializing, and resetting the project.

If two media files are selected in the administrative window, one with continuous and one with discrete time domain, the combined editor can be started. Each page of the discrete medium can be associated with a certain time position of the continuous medium. The time position of individual pages can be adjusted with a mouse drag. The actual time position is shown by a vertical red line in the editor window.

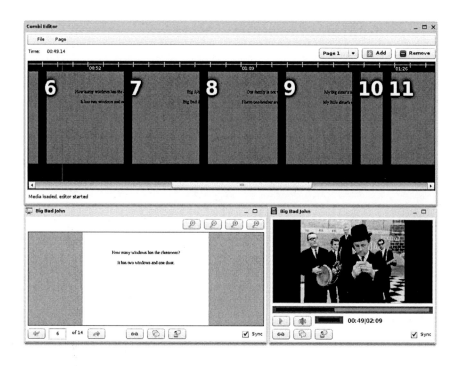

Figure A.15: Combined editor windows.

Appendix B

The Server

This appendix describes the prerequisites, installation, and operation of the server. The README file also contains version specific installation instructions for the system administrator.

B.1   Prerequisites

For proper operation, several additional Perl modules are required. For Ubuntu systems, these modules are prepared separately as native packages. These can be easily installed with the `apt-get` command. The following list reflects the packages used in Ubuntu 12.04 (Precise Pangolin).

```
libdbi-perl
libdbd-pg-perl
libfilesys-df-perl
libarchive-any-perl
libarchive-zip-perl
libxml-simple-perl
libthreads-perl
libthreads-shared-perl
libhtml-template-perl
libclass-method-modifiers-perl
libregexp-common-perl
libregexp-common-email-address-perl
```

Packages which are not standardly available in the Ubuntu distribution are placed in the `extra` subdirectory and have to be compiled and installed manually.

SWFtools are required for the transformation of the input PDF files during the import process. SWFtools is a suite of manipulation programs that comes either in the binary form or it can be downloaded in the source form and compiled manually. Currently, the pdf2swf is the only program used from the whole suite.

In case of manual compilation, following packages are required:

```
zlib1g-dev
libgif-dev
libfreetype6-dev
libjpeg8-dev
g++
```

B.2   Installation

The server software comes in form of a tar archive which can be extracted using the standard commands. After unpacking, there is a `config.inc.sample` file in the main directory. This file can be used as a template for the real configuration file `config.inc`. The configuration file itself is written in Perl and it has to be syntactically correct. Listing B.1 shows the configuration file template. Purpose of each item is briefly described in the listing using Perl comments.

Listing B.1: Configuration file template.

```perl
use utf8;

# Server name
our $name = 'OLS Development';

# Optional alias for STDERR log messages
our $alias = 'devel';

# SMTP server for mail notifications
our $smtp_server = 'my.smtp.mail.server.com';

# Originating email address for notifications
our $email = 'admin.email@localhost';

# Local path of the media directory
our $media_dir = '/opt/ols/media';

# Path to swftools binaries
our $swftools_dir = '/usr/src/swftools';

# Directory for incoming uploads
our $upload_dir = '/opt/ols/upload';
```

```perl
# List of authentication methods (their aliases)
# to try in order of preference
our @auth_methods = qw(local ldap ldap2 ilias);

# Configuration hash for authentication methods.
# Refer to each module for specific settings.
our %auth_config = (
    local => { module => 'local', description => 'local system
        users' },
    ldap  => {
        regex         => "^pa\.",
        module        => 'ldap',
        autoadd       => 1,
        description   => 'studip authentication',
        defaultrole   => 'passau',
        base_dn       => 'o=uni-pa',
        ldap_uri      => 'ldaps://my.ldap.host1.com',
        ldap_pw_expired => 'Password expired, please, change it '
                      .'<a href="https://server.com/passwd">here</a
                      >.',
    },
    ldap2 => {
        regex         => "^r\.",
        module        => 'ldap',
        autoadd       => 1,
        description   => 'studip authentication',
        defaultrole   => 'regensburg',
        base_dn       => "o=uni-r",
    },
    ilias => {
        regex         => "^vhb\.",
        module        => 'ilias',
        autoadd       => 1,
        description   => 'vhb authentication against vhb.uni-passau
            .de',
        rolemap       => { AuthorWi2 => 'admin' }
    },
);

# General server configuration, DB, log file, etc.
our %config = (
    db_host  => 'localhost',
    db_name  => 'database_name',
    db_port  => 5432,
    db_user  => 'user',
    db_pass  => 'password',
    log_file => '/opt/ols/server.log',
    motd     => 'Banner message',
    socket   => '/opt/ols/wipc',
);
```

```
# URL path to gateway script for downloading uplink configuration
our $http_gw = 'http://url-path-to-core.pl/';

# Information regarding the uplink connection
our %uplink = (
    host     => 'my.uplink.host.com',
    port     => 3006,
    secport  => 3005,
);

# Configuration describing all access nodes of the cloud
our @uplink_nodes = (
    \%uplink,
    );
```

The syntax check of modified configuration file can be performed with

```
# perl -c config.inc
config.inc syntax OK
```

B.2.1 Authentication

The server includes the extended authentication component which allows multiple concurrent authentication methods. Individual authentication modules are located in the `OLS/Auth` directory. Upon arrival of the user credentials consisting of name and password, the server tries to find the appropriate authentication method and tries to perform the authentication.

The configuration of every authentication method is specified in the `%auth_config` hash. The `module` determines which Perl module should be loaded and used for the authentication process. The optional `regex` variable specifies the mandatory pattern used for the proper method recognition. In case that the name matches with the `regex`, the same regular expression is also used for substitution with an empty string. The stripped name is then used for the authentication.

All authentication methods are used in the order of preference which is specified in the `@auth_methods` array.

B.2.2 Web Server

The web server plays the essential role for safe authentication over HTTPS and file downloads. Any server with CGI support can be used. The `core.pl` file in the main directory must be accessible through the web server as a CGI script. Note that use of HTTPS is mandatory for safe communication and transmission of user credentials. Place the compiled binaries of the client application (`OLS.swf` and `Console.swf`) in the same directory with `core.pl`.

B.2.3 Initialization

If the database does not already exist, it can be created and initialized with the following command:

```
# ./server.pl --createdb
```

After that, there should be at least one administrative user account. Administrative users can be added with the -addadmin option. This option creates new users and assigns roles *admin* and *superadmin* to them. The *admin* role is mandatory for loading of the administrative module and content manipulation, the *superadmin* role is mandatory for the maintenance of user accounts and roles.

```
# ./server.pl --addadmin admin:password
```

After a proper configuration and addition of administrative users, the server can be started.

```
# ./server.pl
```

The server process writes notifications to the standard output and into the log file. The verbosity level can be adjusted with the -verbose option. Without an argument, the option turns on the verbosity of all modules. Optional argument containing a regular expression can be used to turn on the verbosity of selected modules. For example, the following invocation turns on the verbosity of all authentication modules:

```
# ./server --verbose=^OLS::Auth::
```

Increased verbosity comes in very handy during the development of further modules and also in initial setup stages.

B.3 Operation

Properly configured, the server fills the internal in-memory database with the content of the configured PostgreSQL database. After several integrity checks, the server starts accepting incoming client connections. The server application can be terminated with a TERM signal.

Bibliography

[1] B.B. Agarwal, S.P. Tayal, and M. Gupta. *Software Engineering and Testing.* Computer science series. Jones & Bartlett Learning, 2009.

[2] J. Angelus. *Bigbluebutton.* Duct Publishing, 2012.

[3] Panos J. Antsaklis. A brief introduction to the theory and applications of hybrid systems, 2000.

[4] J.R. Balfour, M. Shaw, and N. Bremer. *Advanced Photovoltaic System Design.* The Art and Science of Photovoltaics. Jones & Bartlett Learning, 2011.

[5] T. Berners-Lee, R. Fielding, and H. Frystyk. Hypertext Transfer Protocol – HTTP/1.0. RFC 1945 (Informational), May 1996.

[6] H. Bidgoli. *The internet encyclopedia: A-F.* Number Bd. 1 in The internet encyclopedia: A-F. John Wiley & Sons Australia, Limited, 2004.

[7] Barry W. Boehm. A spiral model of software development and enhancement. *Computer*, 21(5):61–72, May 1988.

[8] André B. Bondi. Characteristics of scalability and their impact on performance. In *Proceedings of the 2nd international workshop on Software and performance*, WOSP '00, pages 195–203, New York, NY, USA, 2000. ACM.

[9] D. Butenhof. *Programming with POSIX(R) Threads.* Addison-Wesley Professional Computing Series. ADDISON WESLEY Publishing Company Incorporated, 1997.

[10] Tim Carmody. 30 billion watts and rising: balancing the internet's energy and infrastructure needs. http://www.theverge.com/2012/9/23/3377868/cloud-internet-infrastructure-waste-energy-new-york-times, 2012. [Online; accessed 15-Apr-2013].

[11] R.H. Carver and K.C. Tai. *Modern Multithreading: Implementing, Testing, and Debugging Multithreaded Java and C++/Pthreads/Win32 Programs.* Wiley, 2005.

[12] L.N. Cassel and R.H. Austing. *Computer Networks and Open Systems: An Application Development Perspective.* Jones and Bartlett Publishers, 2000.

[13] Julien Cervelle, Rémi Forax, Gautier Loyauté, and Gilles Roussel. Banzai: a java framework for the implementation of high-performance servers. In *Proceedings of the 2009 ACM symposium on Applied Computing*, SAC '09, pages 1903–1909, New York, NY, USA, 2009. ACM.

[14] T. Christiansen, L. Wall, brian foy, and J. Orwant. *Programming Perl: Unmatched Power for Text Processing and Scripting.* Oreilly Series. O'Reilly Media, Incorporated, 2012.

[15] Carlos J. Costa and Manuela Aparicio. Analysis of e-learning processes. In *Proceedings of the 2011 Workshop on Open Source and Design of Communication*, OSDOC '11, pages 37–40, New York, NY, USA, 2011. ACM.

[16] A. Curioso, R. Bradford, and P. Galbraith. *Expert PHP and MySQL.* Wrox expert one-on-one. Wiley, 2010.

[17] Michael Dale and Sally M. Benson. Energy Balance of the Global Photovoltaic (PV) Industry - Is the PV Industry a Net Electricity Producer? *Environ. Sci. Technol.*, 47(7):3482–3489, February 2013.

[18] S. Deering and R. Hinden. Internet Protocol, Version 6 (IPv6) Specification. RFC 2460 (Draft Standard), December 1998. Updated by RFCs 5095, 5722, 5871, 6437, 6564.

[19] A. Der Minassians and Berkeley University of California. *Stirling Engines for Low-temperature Solar-thermal-electric Power Generation.* University of California, Berkeley, 2007.

[20] O. Dubuisson. *ASN.1: Communication Between Heterogeneous Systems.* Academic Press, Incorporated, 2001.

[21] Y. Fain, V. Rasputnis, and A. Tartakovsky. *Enterprise Development with Flex: Best Practices for RIA Developers.* O'Reilly Media, 2010.

[22] I. Fette and A. Melnikov. The WebSocket Protocol. RFC 6455 (Proposed Standard), December 2011.

[23] R. Fielding, J. Gettys, J. Mogul, H. Frystyk, L. Masinter, P. Leach, and T. Berners-Lee. Hypertext Transfer Protocol – HTTP/1.1. RFC 2616 (Draft Standard), June 1999. Updated by RFCs 2817, 5785, 6266, 6585.

[24] Roy Thomas Fielding and Gail E. Kaiser. The apache http server project. *IEEE Internet Computing*, 1(4):88–90, 1997.

[25] Joseph Flaherty. Raspberry pi quickly approaches 1 million units sold. http://www.wired.com/design/2013/01/raspberry-pi-million-boards/, 2013. [Online; accessed 15-Apr-2013].

[26] Анатолий Гришаев. Storable::amf3 perl module. http://search.cpan.org/~grian/Storable-AMF/, 2011. Version 1.00.

[27] B. Gallmeister. *POSIX.4 Programmers Guide: Programming for the Real World*. Oreilly Series. O'Reilly Media, Incorporated, 1995.

[28] G. Giambene. *Queuing Theory and Telecommunications: Networks and Applications*. Springer, 2005.

[29] A. Goldsetin, E. Weyl, and L. Lazaris. *HTML5 and CSS3 for the Real World*. SitePoint Pty. Limited, 2011.

[30] J.S. Gray. *Interprocess Communications in Linux*. Prentice Hall, 2003.

[31] R. Grove. *Web Based Application Development*. Jones & Bartlett Learning, 2009.

[32] Carl A. Gutwin, Michael Lippold, and T. C. Nicholas Graham. Real-time groupware in the browser: testing the performance of web-based networking. In *Proceedings of the ACM 2011 conference on Computer supported cooperative work*, CSCW '11, pages 167–176, New York, NY, USA, 2011. ACM.

[33] David Hauger and Mirkam Köck. State of the art of adaptivity in e-learning platforms, 2007.

[34] B. Holmes and J. Gardner. *E-Learning: Concepts and Practice*. SAGE Publications, 2006.

[35] P. Isaias, Kinshuk, and D. Ifenthaler. *Towards Learning and Instruction in Web 3.0*. SpringerLink : Bücher. Springer New York, 2012.

[36] D. Josephsen. *Building a Monitoring Infrastructure with Nagios*. Pearson Education, 2007.

[37] Evelyn Kigozi Kahiigi, Love Ekenberg, Henrik Hansson, F.F Tusubira, and Mats Danielson. Exploring the e-learning state of art. *EJEL*, 6(2), 2008.

[38] S. Keagy. *Integrating voice and data networks*. Cisco Core Series. Cisco Press, 2000.

[39] P. Kleinschmidt and C. Rank. *Relationale Datenbanksysteme: Eine praktische Einführung*. Springer, 2004.

[40] J. Klensin. Simple Mail Transfer Protocol. RFC 5321 (Draft Standard), October 2008.

[41] Jonathan G Koomey. Estimating total power consumption by servers in the us and the world, 2007.

[42] Janne Kuuskeri and Tommi Mikkonen. Partitioning web applications between the server and the client. In *Proceedings of the 2009 ACM symposium on Applied Computing*, SAC '09, pages 647–652, New York, NY, USA, 2009. ACM.

[43] M.R. Lee and M.F. Gaffney. *Leading a Digital School: Principles and Practice*. Acer Press, 2008.

[44] F. Lehner. *Wissensmanagement: Grundlagen, Methoden und technische Unterstützung*. Hanser : Kompetenz gewinnt. Hanser Fachbuchverlag, 2009.

[45] G. Lembke and G.L. andere. *Wissensnetzwerke*. LearnAct!, 2006.

[46] S. Loreto, P. Saint-Andre, S. Salsano, and G. Wilkins. Known Issues and Best Practices for the Use of Long Polling and Streaming in Bidirectional HTTP. RFC 6202 (Informational), April 2011.

[47] John C. McCallum. Memory prices (1957-2013). http://www.jcmit.com/memoryprice.htm, 2013. [Online; accessed 15-Apr-2013].

[48] C. Moock. *Essential ActionScript 3.0*. O'Reilly Media, 2008.

[49] D. Moore, R. Budd, and E. Benson. *Professional Rich Internet Applications: AJAX and Beyond*. Wrox professional guides. Wiley, 2007.

[50] Daisuke Murase. Data::amf perl module. http://search.cpan.org/~typester/Data-AMF-0.09/, 2010. Version 0.09.

[51] Traian Nicula. Xml socket server applications as an alternative for simulation interoperability. In *Proceedings of the 2007 summer computer simulation conference*, SCSC, pages 1163–1170, San Diego, CA, USA, 2007. Society for Computer Simulation International.

[52] J. Nielsen and K. Pernice. *Eyetracking Web Usability*. Voices That Matter. Pearson Education, 2010.

[53] J. Noble, T. Anderson, G. Braithwaite, M. Casario, and R. Tretola. *Flex 4 Cookbook: Real-world recipes for developing Rich Internet Applications*. O'Reilly Media, 2010.

[54] M. Novák, V. Přenosil, M. Svítek, and Z. Votruba. *Problémy spolehlivosti, životnosti a beypečnosti systémů*. Edice monografií NNW. České vysoké učení technické v Praze, Fakulta dopravní, 2005.

[55] M. Novák, Z. Votruba, and J. Faber. *Problems of Reliability in Interactions Between Human Subjects and Artificial Systems: (first Book on Microsleeps)*. Edice monografií NNW. České vysoké učení technické v Praze, Fakulta dopravní, 2004.

[56] J. Oikarinen and D. Reed. Internet Relay Chat Protocol. RFC 1459 (Experimental), May 1993. Updated by RFCs 2810, 2811, 2812, 2813.

[57] Lucian Popa, Ali Ghodsi, and Ion Stoica. Http as the narrow waist of the future internet. In *Proceedings of the 9th ACM SIGCOMM Workshop on Hot Topics in Networks*, Hotnets-IX, pages 6:1–6:6, New York, NY, USA, 2010. ACM.

[58] J. Postel. User Datagram Protocol. RFC 768 (Standard), August 1980.

[59] J. Postel. Internet Protocol. RFC 791 (Standard), September 1981. Updated by RFCs 1349, 2474.

[60] J. Postel. Transmission Control Protocol. RFC 793 (Standard), September 1981. Updated by RFCs 1122, 3168, 6093, 6528.

[61] K.A. Robbins and S. Robbins. *Unix Systems Programming: Communication, Concurrency and Threads*. Prentice Hall, 2003.

[62] J. Russell and R. Cohn. *Ilias*. Book on Demand, 2012.

[63] J. Russell and R. Cohn. *Thttpd*. Book on Demand, 2012.

[64] W. Sanders and C. Cumaranatunge. *ActionScript 3.0 Design Patterns: Object Oriented Programming Techniques*. O'Reilly Media, 2008.

[65] K.J. Schäfer. *Internetportal für eine Virtuelle Hochschule.: Entwicklung einer Plattform für Learning on Demand. Dissertation*. Gabler Edition Wissenschaft. Deutscher Universitätsvlg, 2001.

[66] Cecil Schmidt, Justin Higgins, and Lance Gliser. Implementation of an interactive web application using foss, a participant-oriented evaluation study. *J. Comput. Sci. Coll.*, 22(4):22–28, April 2007.

[67] R. Shanmugam, R. Padmini, and S. Nivedita. *Special Edition Using Tcp/Ip*. Special Edition Series. Que Pub., 2002.

[68] George Siemens. Connectivism: A learning theory for the digital age. In *International Journal of Instructional Technology and Distance Learning*, 2005.

[69] B. Sosinsky. *Networking Bible*. Bible Series. Wiley, 2009.

[70] C. Stary. *Interaktive Systeme.: Software-Entwicklung und Software-Ergonomie*. Vieweg Informatik, Wirtschaftsinformatik. Vieweg Friedr. + Sohn Ver, 1996.

[71] L. Stein. *Network Programming With Perl*. ADDISON WESLEY Publishing Company Incorporated, 2001.

[72] W.R. Stevens, B. Fenner, and A.M. Rudoff. *UNIX Network Programming*. Number Bd. 1 in Addison-Wesley Professional Computing Series. Addison-Wesley, 2004.

[73] R. Stones and N. Matthew. *Beginning Databases with PostgreSQL: From Novice to Professional*. The expert's voice in open source. Apress, 2005.

[74] G. Utas. *Robust Communications Software: Extreme Availability, Reliability and Scalability for Carrier-Grade Systems*. Wiley, 2005.

[75] S. Voida and Georgia Institute of Technology. *Exploring User Interface Challenges in Supporting Activity-based Knowledge Work Practices*. Georgia Institute of Technology, 2008.

[76] J.M. Voogt and G.A. Knezek. *International handbook of information technology in primary and secondary education*. Number Teil 1 in Springer international handbook of information technology in primary and secondary education. Springer Science+Business Media, LLC, 2008.

[77] P. Wainwright. *Pro Perl*. Expert's Voice in Open Source. Apress, 2005.

[78] Wikipedia. Apache flex. http://en.wikipedia.org/wiki/Apache_Flex, 2013. [Online; accessed 13-Feb-2013].

[79] Wikipedia. Load (computing). http://en.wikipedia.org/wiki/Load_(computing), 2013. [Online; accessed 11-Feb-2013].

[80] WWW. Action message format – amf 3. http://opensource.adobe.com/wiki/download/attachments/1114283/amf3_spec_05_05_08.pdf, 2002–2006. [Online; accessed 18-Apr-2013].

[81] WWW. Actionscript 3, language specification. http://livedocs.adobe.com/specs/actionscript/3, 2006. [Online; accessed 18-Apr-2013].

[82] WWW. Apache flex®. `http://flex.apache.org/`, 2013. The open-source framework for building expressive web and mobile applications.

[83] WWW. The comprehensive perl archive network – www.cpan.org. `http://cpan.org/`, 2013. [Online; accessed 21-Feb-2013].

[84] WWW. Db-engines ranking. `http://db-engines.com/en/ranking`, 2013. [Online; accessed 15-Apr-2013].

[85] WWW. Freecode. `http://freecode.com/`, 2013. [Online; accessed 29-May-2013].

[86] WWW. Ilias learning management system. `http://www.ilias.de/`, 2013. [Online; accessed 29-May-2013].

[87] WWW. Statistics | adobe flash runtimes. `http://www.adobe.com/products/flashruntimes/statistics.html`, 2013. [Online; accessed 18-Apr-2013].

[88] WWW. Usage of web servers for websites. `http://w3techs.com/technologies/overview/web_server/all`, 2013. [Online; accessed 15-Apr-2013].